God's
Little Book™
of Answers to
Big Questions

GOD'S little book OF ANSWERS TO BIG questions

AMY E. MASON

GENERAL EDITOR

TYNDALE HOUSE PUBLISHERS, INC.

CAROL STREAM, ILLINOIS

LIVING
EXPRESSIONS
COLLECTION

Living Expressions invites you to explore
God's Word in a way that is refreshing to
the spirit and restorative to the soul.

Visit Tyndale online at www.tyndale.com.

TYNDALE, Tyndale's quill logo, *Living Expressions*, and the Living
Expressions logo are registered trademarks of Tyndale House Publishers,
Inc. *God's Little Book* is a trademark of Tyndale House Publishers, Inc.

God's Little Book of Answers to Big Questions

Copyright © 2020 by Ronald A. Beers. All rights reserved.

General editor: Amy E. Mason.

Contributing editors: Ronald A. Beers and Katherine J. Butler

Cover and interior images are the property of their respective copyright
holders, and all rights are reserved. Fabric texture © SPIN/Adobe Stock;
hand-drawn decoration © Julia Henze/Shutterstock; palm leaf pattern ©
De-V/Shutterstock; floral bouquet © lilett/Adobe Stock.

Designed by Nicole Grimes

Scripture quotations are taken from the *Holy Bible*, New Living
Translation, copyright © 1996, 2004, 2015 by Tyndale House
Foundation. Used by permission of Tyndale House Publishers, Inc.,
Carol Stream, Illinois 60188. All rights reserved.

For information about special discounts for bulk purchases, please
contact Tyndale House Publishers at csresponse@tyndale.com, or call
1-800-323-9400.

ISBN 978-1-4964-1811-1

Printed in China

26   25   24   23   22   21   20
7   6   5   4   3   2   1

TABLE OF CONTENTS

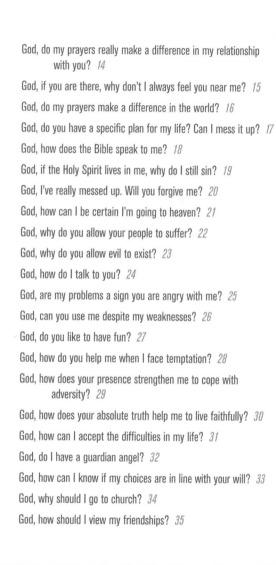

INTRODUCTION

WHETHER YOUR FAITH IN GOD is new or you've known him for a long time, you may have questions about who he is and what he wants for your life. God invites you to bring your questions to him.

God's Little Book of Answers to Big Questions provides a quick and easy way to find answers to 150 big and challenging questions asked by believers and unbelievers alike—such as "God, why do you allow your people to suffer?" and "God, what does it mean to be holy?"

The questions and answers can be used as devotional readings, as a reference guide, or as a resource to help others who have questions about how faith in God works out practically in our daily lives. You can search the table of contents for questions you may have about God, or you can just start reading from the beginning. Every question comes with an answer from the Bible, a short devotional reading to add context, and a promise from God.

As you read the questions and answers, pray that the Holy Spirit will speak to you, opening your heart to his guidance and wisdom, and that your faith will be strengthened and encouraged. We hope this little book has a *big* impact on your life.

God, how can I know you are there?

[Jesus replied,] "I will ask the Father, and he will give you another Advocate, who will never leave you." JOHN 14:16

One of God's greatest assurances is that he is with you. If you have a relationship with his Son, Jesus, you have received the future promise of eternal life on God's new earth. And you also receive another gift—the immediate and constant presence of God's Spirit, also called the Holy Spirit or the Advocate. This is God himself, living in you. God's presence is a guarantee to those who sincerely follow Jesus, believing that all he said and did are true. Once the Holy Spirit comes to live within you, he will never leave you. This is a promise you can cling to, even when God seems far away.

GOD'S PROMISE TO YOU Don't be afraid, for I am with you. Don't be discouraged, for I am your God. ISAIAH 41:10

God, why don't I feel close to you sometimes?

ANSWER FROM GOD'S WORD The LORD's arm is not too weak to save you, nor is his ear too deaf to hear you call. It's your sins that have cut you off from God. ISAIAH 59:1-2

Sin can disrupt your connection with God. When you knowingly persist in sinful attitudes and behaviors (not living in obedience to God and his Word), your heart becomes hardened, making God seem distant. Obedience (doing what God says in his Word) allows God to lead you along the best pathway for your life and the way to eternal life with him. An open heart and willingness to say *yes* to God is a step of obedience that moves you closer to him.

GOD'S PROMISE TO YOU You will show me the way of life, granting me the joy of your presence and the pleasures of living with you forever. PSALM 16:11

God, is the universe the result of a random event, or was it created for a reason?

ANSWER FROM GOD'S WORD In the beginning God created the heavens and the earth. GENESIS 1:1

The universe is no accident, and neither are you. God's love for the world, and for you, existed even before the earth was formed. Everything was made for God's glory, and you were made to have companionship with him and to worship him, loving and delighting in his holiness and pointing others to enjoy his glory as the ultimate reason for living. Don't get hung up on *how* God made the universe, but simply recognize that he made it intentionally out of love. That's how much he values you.

GOD'S PROMISE TO YOU The LORD merely spoke, and the heavens were created. He breathed the word, and all the stars were born. . . . The LORD's plans stand firm forever; his intentions can never be shaken. PSALM 33:6, 11

God, do you care about me?

ANSWER FROM GOD'S WORD   I care about you, and I will pay attention to you. . . . Give all your worries and cares to God, for he cares about you.
EZEKIEL 36:9; 1 PETER 5:7

You are important to God, and he cares deeply for you. He wants to walk with you through your problems and rejoice with you in your celebrations. His love pursues you, even before you have voiced your needs. Because God cares about you, he invites you to give your worries to him in exchange for his peace. This is a daily grace for you because you are his child. He promises both to pay attention to your needs and to pursue you with goodness and a love that never fails.

GOD'S PROMISE TO YOU   I still belong to you; you hold my right hand. You guide me with your counsel, leading me to a glorious destiny.
PSALM 73:23-24

God, do you really talk to people?

ANSWER FROM GOD'S WORD My sheep listen to my voice; I know them, and they follow me. JOHN 10:27

Relationships require conversation—both listening and speaking. God is always ready to listen, but there are also many ways in which he initiates conversation with you. Here are just a few: prayer, Bible reading, worship, song, the inspiration of nature, and the wisdom of other godly people. Many people don't think to listen to God during these times or pause long enough to make space for him. If you expect God to speak in a particular way, you may miss it when he speaks to you in another way. God wants to speak to you. Are you listening?

GOD'S PROMISE TO YOU You can be sure of this: The LORD set apart the godly for himself. The LORD will answer when I call to him. PSALM 4:3

God, where is heaven?

We are fully confident, and we would rather be away from these earthly bodies, for then we will be at home with the Lord. 2 CORINTHIANS 5:8

Through the inspiration of the Holy Spirit, the apostle Paul assures believers that when they die they will be truly at home, in the very presence of God the Father and Jesus the Son. Heaven is where Jesus Christ lives and sits on the throne. Right now, we don't know where that is, but the Bible speaks of a new heaven and a new earth, a re-creation and restoration of the universe, coinciding with Jesus' return to judge humankind once and for all. With the coming of the new heaven and new earth, God's home will be with his people—for all eternity. In the meantime, all who have trusted Jesus as Lord will see him at once when they die. Can you imagine the overwhelming joy the moment you arrive in heaven and see Jesus face to face?

GOD'S PROMISE TO YOU Look, God's home is now among his people! He will live with them, and they will be his people. God himself will be with them. REVELATION 21:3

7

God, how can you allow people to go to hell?

ANSWER FROM GOD'S WORD Make every effort to be found living peaceful lives that are pure and blameless. . . . And remember, our Lord's patience gives people time to be saved. 2 PETER 3:14-15

Hell was made for Satan, his demons, and people who reject God. God doesn't *send* people to hell; people *choose* to go. Humanly speaking, it is impossible for us to live up to God's standards. Our willful rebellion—called *sin*—has the dire consequence of separating us from God. God is always just and holy; when we sin, we are unjust and unholy. Unjust and unholy people cannot live in a perfect heaven. But our loving and merciful God provides us with a rescue plan: If we will acknowledge our sin and rebellion and follow Jesus, he will wipe away our sin—by his death on the cross and his resurrection—and make us just and holy in God's eyes. Then we will receive the wonderful gift of eternal life with him in a perfect future world. All are invited to take part in this rescue plan, but not everyone will accept it. Will you?

GOD'S PROMISE TO YOU Nothing can ever separate us from God's love. . . . Not even the powers of hell. ROMANS 8:38

God, what does it mean to have a sinful nature?

ANSWER FROM GOD'S WORD When Adam sinned, sin entered the world. Adam's sin brought death, so death spread to everyone, for everyone sinned. ROMANS 5:12

When God breathed life into Adam and Eve, they became distinct from any other creature. God gave them a conscience and the ability to both reason and love. But these gifts came with the capacity to choose—to do good or evil, to love or hate. This ability to choose is called free will; without it, there is no goodness or love. We must *choose* to love, not be *forced* to love. When Adam and Eve disobeyed God, they allowed sin to enter the world, and everything fell under its curse. That corrupted image was passed down from parents to children. Ever since, human beings—exercising their free will—have been prone to do what pleases themselves over what pleases God. But when we choose to follow Jesus, he gives us the indwelling Holy Spirit so we can what pleases God.

GOD'S PROMISE TO YOU Adam's one sin brings condemnation for everyone, but Christ's one act of righteousness brings a right relationship with God and new life for everyone. ROMANS 5:18

God, do you forgive everyone, or just those who believe in you?

ANSWER FROM GOD'S WORD After supper he took another cup of wine and said, "This cup is the new covenant between God and his people—an agreement confirmed with my blood, which is poured out as a sacrifice for you." LUKE 22:20

God loves all people; he created every person who has ever lived, and he knows each one by name. He longs for every person to live with him forever. But he won't force them; that isn't real love. Those who choose to follow him and live according to his rule enter his *covenant love*. In this relationship, believers experience forgiveness of sins and new life to walk in freedom away from those sins. God's covenant love brings both the guarantee of salvation and the ongoing forgiveness we need to live in obedience to him.

GOD'S PROMISE TO YOU Believe in the Lord Jesus and you will be saved. ACTS 16:31

God, can believing in Jesus really change my life?

ANSWER FROM GOD'S WORD I pray that from his glorious, unlimited resources he will empower you with inner strength through his Spirit.
EPHESIANS 3:16

Before we commit to following Jesus, we are operating only in our own strength. After we begin a personal relationship with Jesus, we become filled with his Holy Spirit, and the very life and power of God dwell in us. God uses many avenues to transform our thinking and thus our actions. The change comes not from ourselves but from the awesome power of God within us. We become new people, and we continue to be renewed from our old sinful nature as we come to know Jesus more and more.

GOD'S PROMISE TO YOU Anyone who belongs to Christ has become a new person. The old life is gone; a new life has begun! 2 CORINTHIANS 5:17

God, what does it mean that I have power as a follower of Jesus?

ANSWER FROM GOD'S WORD You will receive power when the Holy Spirit comes upon you.
ACTS 1:8

As a follower of Jesus, you have real power through the Holy Spirit. Satan wants to make you feel weak and defeated. But because of the Holy Spirit, you are not without resources! God's power—the wisdom that formed the world and the strength that raised Jesus from the dead—is available to you. You may feel defeated by your weaknesses and struggles, but God's power has already overcome it all. He offers divine strength and wisdom to those who have surrendered to him for the purpose of glorifying him.

GOD'S PROMISE TO YOU With God's help we will do mighty things. PSALM 60:12

God, why are Christians encouraged to share their faith with others?

ANSWER FROM GOD'S WORD He told them, "Go into all the world and preach the Good News to everyone." MARK 16:15

God wants the world to hear the Good News that he loves everyone and sent his Son, Jesus, to rescue them from spiritual death so they can enjoy eternal life with him. Sharing our faith is simply living our lives in a way that models Jesus' life and bears witness to how we've seen God at work in us. The strength of your testimony comes from the power of God at work in you. It's not up to you to transform others; God does the work of redemption as you allow him to work through you to share Jesus with others. You can rely on him to act because he wants everyone to hear the Good News.

GOD'S PROMISE TO YOU This same Good News that came to you is going out all over the world. It is bearing fruit everywhere by changing lives, just as it changed your lives from the day you first heard and understood the truth about God's wonderful grace. COLOSSIANS 1:6

God, do my prayers really make a difference in my relationship with you?

ANSWER FROM GOD'S WORD I love the LORD because he hears my voice and my prayer for mercy. Because he bends down to listen, I will pray as long as I have breath! PSALM 116:1-2

Through prayer, you connect to the one true God in holy conversation. This kind of connection is life changing. The deeper your relationship with God, the more you will experience and recognize his power and presence in your life and in the world. As you release your burdens to God, praise him for what he's done, and ask him to show you his work all around you, he will fill you with his peace and with confidence in your faith.

GOD'S PROMISE TO YOU When you pray, I will listen. If you look for me wholeheartedly, you will find me. JEREMIAH 29:12-13

God, if you are there, why don't I always feel you near me?

ANSWER FROM GOD'S WORD Be sure of this: I am with you always, even to the end of the age. MATTHEW 28:20

Sometimes God seems far away when we are in a difficult season and our troubles are overwhelming. If we believe that our hardships are a sign of God's disapproval or his neglect, we will naturally feel abandoned or forgotten. In these moments, remember the truth proclaimed in God's Word: "I am with you always." Even when God seems distant, Scripture reminds us to trust in his promises more than our feelings.

GOD'S PROMISE TO YOU I have cared for you since you were born. Yes, I carried you before you were born. I will be your God throughout your lifetime—until your hair is white with age. I made you, and I will care for you. I will carry you along and save you. ISAIAH 46:3-4

God, do my prayers make a difference in the world?

ANSWER FROM GOD'S WORD The earnest prayer of a righteous person has great power and produces wonderful results. JAMES 5:16

Your prayers really do make a difference. The apostle Paul, who wrote much of the New Testament under the inspiration of the Holy Spirit, often urged believers to pray for others because he had experienced the power of prayer and the impact of a group of praying believers. The Bible is full of examples of how one person's fervent prayer changed the course of events. God hears your prayers and they matter!

GOD'S PROMISE TO YOU I urge you, first of all, to pray for all people. Ask God to help them; intercede on their behalf, and give thanks for them. . . . This is good and pleases God our Savior, who wants everyone to be saved and to understand the truth. 1 TIMOTHY 2:1, 3-4

God, do you have a specific plan for my life? Can I mess it up?

ANSWER FROM GOD'S WORD The LORD will work out his plans for my life. . . . God's gifts and his call can never be withdrawn. PSALM 138:8; ROMANS 11:29

God's plan for your life is not a written script that you must follow; rather, it is a journey with some important destinations and appointments, and a great deal of freedom in the pace and scope of the travel. There are no mistakes that God cannot redeem and use for his plans and purposes. God's plan will always have a sense of mystery to it, but as you seek his guidance, you can be certain that he will lead you on your journey.

GOD'S PROMISE TO YOU God causes everything to work together for the good of those who love God and are called according to his purpose for them. ROMANS 8:28

God, how does the Bible speak to me?

ANSWER FROM GOD'S WORD All Scripture is inspired by God and is useful to teach us what is true and to make us realize what is wrong in our lives. It corrects us when we are wrong and teaches us to do what is right. God uses it to prepare and equip his people to do every good work. 2 TIMOTHY 3:16-17

God's Word speaks truth, helping us recognize the lies that Satan constantly whispers in our ears. It speaks correction, revealing sin and leading us to repentance. It speaks instruction and wisdom, helping us recognize truth and apply it well. God's Word speaks guidance, showing us the right path to take. God's Word speaks hope when we are desperate, comfort when we're hurting, and joy when it's time to celebrate God's victories. Each time you begin to read God's Word, remember that it is living and powerful. Then ask God what he would like to say specifically to you through it.

GOD'S PROMISE TO YOU The word of God is alive and powerful. It is sharper than the sharpest two-edged sword, cutting between soul and spirit, between joint and marrow. It exposes our innermost thoughts and desires. HEBREWS 4:12

God, if the Holy Spirit lives in me, why do I still sin?

ANSWER FROM GOD'S WORD I have discovered . . . that when I want to do what is right, I inevitably do what is wrong. I love God's law with all my heart. But there is another power within me that is at war with my mind. This power makes me a slave to the sin that is still within me. ROMANS 7:21-23

When you make a commitment to follow Jesus, God's Holy Spirit takes up residence in you, giving you freedom from slavery to sin, divine wisdom to live by God's truth, and divine power to live in obedience to God rather than Satan. But the Bible is clear that, as long as you live on this earth, you will have a sinful nature and constantly battle against the temptation to allow sin to control you. Only with the Holy Spirit's help can you win these battles. The struggle to abandon sinful ways is a lifelong process. You will never reach perfection on earth, but by the Spirit's power you can grow in maturity and walk in freedom from slavery to sin. The reward for persevering in faith is eternal life with God, completely free from sin.

GOD'S PROMISE TO YOU Thank God! He gives us victory over sin and death through our Lord Jesus Christ. 1 CORINTHIANS 15:57

God, I've really messed up. Will you forgive me?

ANSWER FROM GOD'S WORD Everyone has sinned; we all fall short of God's glorious standard. Yet God, in his grace, freely makes us right in his sight. He did this through Christ Jesus when he freed us from the penalty for our sins. ROMANS 3:23-24

Forgiveness flows freely from God's generous and merciful heart. You can find forgiveness and peace with God, no matter who you are or what you've done. You must first admit that your actions have fallen short of God's standards and then ask for his forgiveness. When you do, he will faithfully forgive you and help you leave patterns of sin behind you. Forgiveness is always possible for those who truly want a right relationship with God.

GOD'S PROMISE TO YOU Though your sins are like scarlet, I will make them as white as snow. Though they are red like crimson, I will make them as white as wool. ISAIAH 1:18

God, how can I be certain I'm going to heaven?

ANSWER FROM GOD'S WORD This is how God loved the world: He gave his one and only Son, so that everyone who believes in him will not perish but have eternal life. JOHN 3:16

Our certainty of heaven comes through faith that God's plan from the beginning was that Jesus would do what we cannot accomplish ourselves—his death and resurrection overcame the power of death over us and the brokenness caused by sin. The moment you believe this truth, you receive the eternal life he promises.

GOD'S PROMISE TO YOU I am the resurrection and the life. Anyone who believes in me will live, even after dying. JOHN 11:25

God, why do you allow your people to suffer?

ANSWER FROM GOD'S WORD I have told you all this so that you may have peace in me. Here on earth you will have many trials and sorrows. But take heart, because I have overcome the world. JOHN 16:33

Our faith in God doesn't make us immune to troubles or suffering. In fact, Jesus warned that troubles will come. However, we don't suffer alone. We have God's help and the confident hope that one day all our troubles will be redeemed—our bodies will be healed, we will rise to eternal life, and the earth will be renewed, sin erased, and death eradicated. Our struggles won't have the final word, nor will they define our lives, because we walk with the living God, who takes cares of us in our suffering.

GOD'S PROMISE TO YOU Even when I walk through the darkest valley, I will not be afraid, for you are close beside me. PSALM 23:4

God, why do you allow evil to exist?

ANSWER FROM GOD'S WORD You cannot mock the justice of God. You will always harvest what you plant. Those who live only to satisfy their own sinful nature will harvest decay and death from that sinful nature. But those who live to please the Spirit will harvest everlasting life. GALATIANS 6:7-8

God is good, loving, and just. He hates evil. In love, he gave humanity the choice to follow him or not. It would be against his nature to force people to obey him. That would be tyranny. God gives us freedom of choice, while still maintaining his sovereignty over all things. But freedom of choice means we also have the freedom to choose rebellion, rejection, and evil. One day, however, God will set up a new order on a new earth where love will exist in the absence of evil. Those who choose not to love God will be eternally separated from him. In the meantime, God exercises his patience, wanting everyone to turn to him before it's too late.

GOD'S PROMISE TO YOU The Lord isn't really being slow about his promise, as some people think. No, he is being patient for your sake. He does not want anyone to be destroyed, but wants everyone to repent. 2 PETER 3:9

God, how do I talk to you?

ANSWER FROM GOD'S WORD When you pray, go away by yourself, shut the door behind you, and pray to your Father in private. Then your Father, who sees everything, will reward you. . . . Pray in the Spirit at all times and on every occasion. Stay alert and be persistent in your prayers for all believers everywhere. MATTHEW 6:6; EPHESIANS 6:18

Prayer is a conversation between you and God. When you talk to a friend, you don't try to sound overly important or use fancy words. You are comfortable, you ask questions, you share what's on your mind, you tell your friend the desires of your heart and affirm your fondness for your relationship. If you've wronged a friend, you go to him or her and ask for forgiveness. Talking to God is talking to your Creator and friend with an open and genuine heart. The more you pray, the more comfortable you will feel in sharing everything with him, and the more you will be able to hear when he talks to you.

GOD'S PROMISE TO YOU The LORD is close to all who call on him, yes, to all who call on him in truth. PSALM 145:18

God, are my problems a sign you are angry with me?

ANSWER FROM GOD'S WORD Can anything ever separate us from Christ's love? Does it mean he no longer loves us if we have trouble or calamity, or are persecuted, or hungry, or destitute, or in danger, or threatened with death? . . . No, despite all these things, . . . nothing in all creation will ever be able to separate us from the love of God that is revealed in Christ Jesus our Lord. ROMANS 8:35, 37, 39

Sometimes our troubles are the natural consequence of sin, but they never put us out of reach of God's love and forgiveness. Our problems are often the result of our living in a world where sin and evil exist. God doesn't abandon you to face your troubles alone. Your struggles can be the very circumstances that reveal how much God loves you. They are opportunities for your faith to grow and for you to experience his love in greater measure.

GOD'S PROMISE TO YOU You, O Lord, are a God of compassion and mercy, slow to get angry and filled with unfailing love and faithfulness. PSALM 86:15

God, can you use me despite my weaknesses?

Moses pleaded with the LORD, "O Lord, I'm not very good with words. I never have been." . . . Then the LORD asked Moses, "Who makes a person's mouth? . . . Now go! I will be with you as you speak, and I will instruct you in what to say." EXODUS 4:10-12

Moses wasn't an eloquent speaker, yet God used him to boldly confront the pharaoh of Egypt and lead the Israelite slaves out of the land of their oppression and into freedom. Moses is an example and hopeful reminder that God can use you, too, to do whatever he calls you to do. When God touches your life, you will be transformed from weakness to strength. Your weakness might make you feel like an empty vessel, but it is actually the perfect opportunity to be filled with God's power. His power is more evident when he uses your weaknesses to accomplish his work.

GOD'S PROMISE TO YOU My grace is all you need. My power works best in weakness. 2 CORINTHIANS 12:9

God, do you like to have fun?

ANSWER FROM GOD'S WORD Go and celebrate with a feast. . . . This is a sacred day. . . . Don't be dejected and sad, for the joy of the Lord is your strength! NEHEMIAH 8:10

God loves fun. He created our bodies to experience pleasure and joy. He made our taste buds to delight in food, and our nerve endings to enjoy touch. In the Old Testament, God set aside times of celebration and rejoicing for the Israelites. He scheduled regular festivals for people's enjoyment. The things we celebrate and enjoy are reminders that God delights in us and wants us to experience joy.

GOD'S PROMISE TO YOU The Lord your God is living among you. He is a mighty savior. He will take delight in you with gladness. With his love, he will calm all your fears. He will rejoice over you with joyful songs. ZEPHANIAH 3:17

God, how do you help me when I face temptation?

ANSWER FROM GOD'S WORD I have hidden your word in my heart, that I might not sin against you. . . . Be strong in the Lord and in his mighty power. PSALM 119:11; EPHESIANS 6:10

Jesus went through tremendous temptation, so he understands the temptations you're experiencing right now. Satan wants you to feel as if no one understands. He's always trying to trick you into believing that the wrong thing is really the right thing. When you face temptation, dive into God's Word and focus your thoughts on the truth that comes only from God. Every temptation you face is addressed somewhere in the Bible, whether directly or indirectly. God will open your eyes to the right path and will give you the power and confidence to choose it. Your willpower is no match for the power of the enemy, but you can be strong using the mighty power of God.

GOD'S PROMISE TO YOU Since he himself has gone through suffering and testing, he is able to help us when we are being tested. HEBREWS 2:18

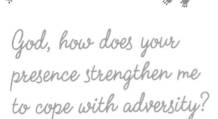

God, how does your presence strengthen me to cope with adversity?

ANSWER FROM GOD'S WORD When you go through deep waters, I will be with you. When you go through rivers of difficulty, you will not drown. When you walk through the fire of oppression, you will not be burned up; the flames will not consume you. ISAIAH 43:2

When going through a time of adversity, have you wondered, *Where is God when I need him most?* Scripture assures us that we will go through deep waters—that, in this life, adversity will come our way. But God gives us hope: He promises to be with us in our troubles, to give us wisdom and understanding, strength to endure, and victory over sin. His presence protects us, comforts us, and strengthens us. Adversity is an important part of the journey. It makes our faith in God stronger and builds our confidence in his promise of a perfect eternal life.

GOD'S PROMISE TO YOU The LORD helps the fallen and lifts those bent beneath their loads. PSALM 145:14

God, how does your absolute truth help me to live faithfully?

In those days Israel had no king; all the people did whatever seemed right in their own eyes. JUDGES 21:25

History is full of examples of individuals who did what was right in their own eyes—with catastrophic consequences for themselves and others. Our culture tells us that we can create our own truth. When truth becomes relative, we live as if we are the god of our own lives. But what happens when one person's truth interferes with another's? There is only one God, the God of the Bible. Living faithfully begins with the admission that he is God—the source of all truth—and you are not. When you live by God's truth, you can be assured that you are doing what is pleasing in his eyes.

Those who love your instructions have great peace and do not stumble. PSALM 119:165

God, how can I accept the difficulties in my life?

ANSWER FROM GOD'S WORD You suffered along with those who were thrown into jail, and when all you owned was taken from you, you accepted it with joy. You knew there were better things waiting for you that will last forever. HEBREWS 10:34

Accepting challenging circumstances doesn't mean giving up; rather, it is a chance to embrace how they will shape and teach you. Your struggles do not define you, but they are part of the story of who you're becoming. Troubles can also increase your hope in the Lord and his promise that everything will be healed and redeemed when he comes to establish the new heaven and the new earth. Drawing strength from God's presence and the hope of heaven can bring you peace in your circumstances today.

GOD'S PROMISE TO YOU I know the LORD is always with me. I will not be shaken, for he is right beside me. PSALM 16:8

God, do I have a guardian angel?

ANSWER FROM GOD'S WORD Angels are only servants—spirits sent to care for people who will inherit salvation. HEBREWS 1:14

Angels are supernatural beings whose main purpose is to worship God and serve him. In the Bible they often perform the role of messengers who deliver God's words to human beings. God uses his angels to counsel, guide, protect, minister to, rescue, fight for, and care for his people. Whether he assigns one specific angel to each person or uses his host of angels is his choice and your blessing. Thank God for the ways in which angels may have touched your life. Chances are that angels have played a greater role than you realize.

GOD'S PROMISE TO YOU He will order his angels to protect you wherever you go. They will hold you up with their hands so you won't even hurt your foot on a stone. PSALM 91:11-12

God, how can I know if my choices are in line with your will?

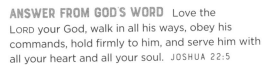

ANSWER FROM GOD'S WORD Love the Lord your God, walk in all his ways, obey his commands, hold firmly to him, and serve him with all your heart and all your soul. JOSHUA 22:5

The best choices you can make are to sincerely love God and others and to live according to the truths and principles found in God's Word. Doing this will always point you toward what pleases God. To help you make good choices—and avoid decisions that benefit yourself at others' expense—read God's Word as often as you can, ask for his guidance in prayer, and listen to the advice of people who are known for godly wisdom. It is a challenge to honor God in every decision, but by obeying him and maintaining a willing attitude, you can trust that the outcome will be pleasing to him.

GOD'S PROMISE TO YOU [The Lord] guides me along right paths, bringing honor to his name. PSALM 23:3

God, why should I go to church?

ANSWER FROM GOD'S WORD The one thing I ask of the LORD—the thing I seek most—is to live in the house of the LORD all the days of my life, delighting in the LORD's perfections and meditating in his Temple. PSALM 27:4

Even though God lives in the heart of every believer, he also lives in the community of the church. When the church is gathered together, God is there in a special way. Participating with other believers in worship is meaningful in a different way than worshiping by yourself. Getting involved in a church is a wonderful way to experience God's love through his family of believers and to witness how he is working in your community and around the world.

GOD'S PROMISE TO YOU [Christ] makes the whole body fit together perfectly. As each part does its own special work, it helps the other parts grow, so that the whole body is healthy and growing and full of love. EPHESIANS 4:16

God, how should I view my friendships?

ANSWER FROM GOD'S WORD If we are living in the light, as God is in the light, then we have fellowship with each other, and the blood of Jesus, his Son, cleanses us from all sin. 1 JOHN 1:7

Good friends are a wonderful gift, but friendship between believers is unique because of their common perspective on life. Friendships with other believers help you grow in your faith as you explore God together. These friends can also come alongside to give you strength and godly wisdom in times of crisis or temptation. Friendships with people who don't believe as you do are also important and beneficial, because God made all people in his image. But friendships with other believers are meant to be an expression of God's love lived out in community.

GOD'S PROMISE TO YOU [Jesus said,] "Where two or three gather together as my followers, I am there among them." MATTHEW 18:20

God, how can my life have the greatest impact?

ANSWER FROM GOD'S WORD There was a believer in Joppa named Tabitha. . . . She was always doing kind things for others and helping the poor. ACTS 9:36

God's influence in your life can be very attractive to others. After all, you have the perfect, loving, caring Holy Spirit living within you to help you love others as Jesus loved. Being a friendly neighbor, volunteering to serve the needy, being a responsible citizen, making peace with difficult people, and treating others with fairness and respect are good ways to influence your community. With God's power, your character can become a beacon of light that brightens the whole community with God's transforming ways. Live your life in such a way that your neighbors can say, "We can plainly see that the LORD is with you" (Genesis 26:28).

GOD'S PROMISE TO YOU [Jesus said,] "You are the light of the world. . . . Let your good deeds shine out for all to see, so that everyone will praise your heavenly Father." MATTHEW 5:14, 16

God, what is the key to contentment in life?

ANSWER FROM GOD'S WORD I have learned how to be content with whatever I have. I know how to live on almost nothing or with everything. I have learned the secret of living in every situation. . . . For I can do everything through Christ, who gives me strength. PHILIPPIANS 4:11-13

Contentment and joy do not come from the pursuit of happiness, pleasure, or material possessions, but from gratitude and intimacy with God, recognizing him as the giver of all gifts in your life. The Bible teaches that you will be most contented when you recognize and embrace God's relentless, unfailing love for you. Then, in times of need, you will be aware of his care for you, and your faith and trust in him will grow. God has promised that his love and grace are sufficient for your contentment. Everything else is a bonus.

GOD'S PROMISE TO YOU You thrill me, LORD, with all you have done for me! I sing for joy because of what you have done. O LORD, what great works you do! PSALM 92:4-5

God, why don't you take away the things I fear most?

ANSWER FROM GOD'S WORD All the believers lifted their voices together in prayer.... "O Lord, hear their threats, and give us, your servants, great boldness in preaching your word." ACTS 4:24, 29

The early church was constantly threatened with persecution. The believers did not pray for the threats to end, but for the courage to face them. Sometimes God will remove the things that frighten you. But more often, the Holy Spirit will give you the boldness to face those threats, even turning them into opportunities for spiritual growth. If God took away everything you feared, there would be no need for hope in your life. Hope helps you see beyond the immediate crisis, causing you to place your current problem, as well as your eternal future, in God's hands.

GOD'S PROMISE TO YOU We can rejoice, too, when we run into problems and trials, for we know that they help us develop endurance. And endurance develops strength of character, and character strengthens our confident hope of salvation. And this hope will not lead to disappointment. For we know how dearly God loves us. ROMANS 5:3-5

God, can I really believe your promise of heavenly riches?

ANSWER FROM GOD'S WORD "No eye has seen, no ear has heard, and no mind has imagined what God has prepared for those who love him." But it was to us that God revealed these things by his Spirit. 1 CORINTHIANS 2:9-10

God's promises that his faithful servants will be rewarded in heaven are as certain as all his other promises. The assurance of eternal life gives you courage and hope for life now and changes the way you make choices every day. This life is not all there is; your eternal life will be blessed beyond what you can imagine. Live today in anticipation of the joys awaiting you in heaven and see how your perspective changes.

GOD'S PROMISE TO YOU Jesus replied, . . . "In the future you will see the Son of Man seated in the place of power at God's right hand and coming on the clouds of heaven." MATTHEW 26:64

God, how can I know you are trustworthy?

ANSWER FROM GOD'S WORD God has given both his promise and his oath. These two things are unchangeable because it is impossible for God to lie. Therefore, we who have fled to him for refuge can have great confidence as we hold to the hope that lies before us. This hope is a strong and trustworthy anchor for our souls.
HEBREWS 6:18-19

God is trustworthy because he tells the truth and keeps his promises. Jesus promised he would rise from the dead, and because he did, you can be assured that every other promise God makes to you will also come true. God's very nature is goodness and truth—he cannot lie. His trustworthy character is described as an anchor for your soul—a promise you can hold on to in any season or storm.

GOD'S PROMISE TO YOU Let us hold tightly without wavering to the hope we affirm, for God can be trusted to keep his promise.
HEBREWS 10:23

God, how can I find true purpose in life?

ANSWER FROM GOD'S WORD I take joy in doing your will, my God, for your instructions are written on my heart. . . . Here now is my final conclusion: Fear God and obey his commands, for this is everyone's duty. PSALM 40:8; ECCLESIASTES 12:13

Discovering God's purpose begins with wholehearted commitment to knowing God and his Word. Your Creator loves you and has invited you to enjoy a rich relationship with him, a relationship that shapes and gives meaning to everything you do. The more you know God and pattern your life after his Word, the more meaningful your life will be. God created you for a purpose, and he wants to help you find joy in being who he made you to be.

GOD'S PROMISE TO YOU I cry out to God Most High, to God who will fulfill his purpose for me. PSALM 57:2

God, what should be my highest priority?

ANSWER FROM GOD'S WORD Jesus replied, "The most important commandment is this: . . . 'Love the LORD your God with all your heart, all your soul, all your mind, and all your strength.'" MARK 12:29-30

If you claim Jesus as Lord, then your relationship with him must be the foundation of all you are and all you do. Your highest priority is to know and love him because his love and his Word give you the energy and the desire to love those around you. Let every part of you pursue the Lord wholeheartedly. The more you love God, the more your other priorities will fall into place.

GOD'S PROMISE TO YOU Wherever your treasure is, there the desires of your heart will also be. LUKE 12:34

God, is there really such a thing as spiritual hunger or thirst?

ANSWER FROM GOD'S WORD Jesus replied, "If you only knew the gift God has for you and who you are speaking to, you would ask me, and I would give you living water." JOHN 4:10

What did Jesus mean by "living water"? Many passages in the Bible speak of thirsting after God as one thirsts for water. God is called the fountain of life and living water. When Jesus said he would give living water that could forever quench a person's thirst, he was revealing himself as the Savior who satisfies the soul's deepest needs and desires. Spiritual hunger and thirst are real, and those longings are meant to point you to the one who is the source of peace and satisfaction.

GOD'S PROMISE TO YOU Taste and see that the LORD is good. PSALM 34:8

God, sometimes I feel so lost. Where do you want me to go next?

ANSWER FROM GOD'S WORD Whether the cloud stayed above the Tabernacle for two days, a month, or a year, the people of Israel stayed in camp and did not move on. But as soon as it lifted, they broke camp and moved on. So they camped or traveled at the LORD's command. NUMBERS 9:22-23

The Israelites traveled and camped as God guided them. When you follow God, you know you are where God wants you, whether you are moving or staying where you are. Direction from God is not just for the next big move. He has a purpose in placing you where you are right now. What does God want you to do today? When he wants you to move, he will make that clear.

GOD'S PROMISE TO YOU You see me when I travel and when I rest at home. You know everything I do. PSALM 139:3

God, how do I know that you truly value my life?

ANSWER FROM GOD'S WORD God created human beings in his own image. In the image of God he created them; male and female he created them. GENESIS 1:27

How affirming to know that God chose to create you in his image. You reflect his glory! In addition, your Creator longs to have a relationship with you. Your life is the story of how God created you and is pursuing you, how he wants to rescue you from sin and spiritual death, and how he wants to restore you to perfection and a relationship with him because you are so valuable in his eyes. When you realize how fully God affirms your value, his love will break through the messages the world sends about who you ought to be and will instead encourage you that you are valuable to God just as you are.

GOD'S PROMISE TO YOU We know what real love is because Jesus gave up his life for us. 1 JOHN 3:16

God, how can I cope with the uncertainties of life?

ANSWER FROM GOD'S WORD Blessed are those who trust in the LORD and have made the LORD their hope and confidence. JEREMIAH 17:7

One thing you can always be certain of is God's love for you. When you go through hard times, it doesn't mean that God has abandoned you. Hard times allow God to reveal his infinite love and care for you. He is the only one you can trust completely without fear of disappointment. What he says is true, and what he does is reliable. Experiencing God's love for you gives you security for today and for eternity.

GOD'S PROMISE TO YOU Oh, the joys of those who trust the LORD, who have no confidence in the proud or in those who worship idols. PSALM 40:4

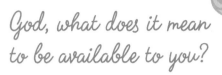

God, what does it mean to be available to you?

ANSWER FROM GOD'S WORD I heard the Lord asking, "Whom should I send as a messenger to this people? Who will go for us?" I said, "Here I am. Send me." *ISAIAH 6:8*

Being available to God means more than just acknowledging his existence. It means reorienting your heart so that your relationship with God affects everything you think, everything you say, and everything you do. You live to serve him. Availability means you have an eagerness to go where he calls you and serve where he places you. It is simply following God with a willing heart. He will bless you—not because of your ability but because of your availability.

GOD'S PROMISE TO YOU Be strong and courageous, and do the work. Don't be afraid or discouraged, for the LORD God, my God, is with you. He will not fail you or forsake you.
1 CHRONICLES 28:20

God, if I'm struggling, can you still use me?

ANSWER FROM GOD'S WORD My dear brothers and sisters, be strong and immovable. Always work enthusiastically for the Lord, for you know that nothing you do for the Lord is ever useless.
1 CORINTHIANS 15:58

You may think your struggles and weaknesses disqualify you from experiencing God's power, but they are actually where his power works best. This power is always meant to glorify God. God ministers to you in your troubles. He transforms your struggles into your greatest effectiveness. God is not waiting for you to be perfect; he's waiting for you to depend on his power to help you through your struggles, to make it clear that it is he who is working through you.

GOD'S PROMISE TO YOU God, who said, "Let there be light in the darkness," has made this light shine in our hearts so we could know the glory of God that is seen in the face of Jesus Christ.
2 CORINTHIANS 4:6

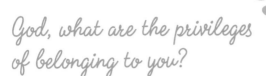

God, what are the privileges of belonging to you?

ANSWER FROM GOD'S WORD Now that you belong to Christ, you are the true children of Abraham. You are his heirs, and God's promise to Abraham belongs to you. GALATIANS 3:29

Belonging to God means you are no longer enslaved to sin; you can overcome it. Belonging to God means you can be certain that you will live eternally with him and receive all he has promised his people in the Bible. On earth, you can experience blessings such as peace of mind and heart, comfort, Christian friendship, and real fulfillment, knowing that you are doing what God has created you to do. As a child of God, you can delight in all the ways he has blessed you.

GOD'S PROMISE TO YOU All praise to God, the Father of our Lord Jesus Christ, who has blessed us with every spiritual blessing in the heavenly realms because we are united with Christ.
EPHESIANS 1:3

God, how can I find security and peace in the midst of change?

ANSWER FROM GOD'S WORD LORD, you remain the same forever! Your throne continues from generation to generation. . . . Jesus Christ is the same yesterday, today, and forever. LAMENTATIONS 5:19; HEBREWS 13:8

If there's one thing you can count on, it's *change*. Sometimes change is expected, even anticipated. Sometimes it is the result of tragedy or unexpected circumstances. Change always rocks the boat of life for a while. During any time of change, it's important to have an anchor and a plan. If your life is anchored to God and your plan is to obey him, true peace is possible no matter what changes come. Because God is unchanging and eternal, obedience to him is the best way to find rock-solid security when you are trying to navigate through troubled waters.

GOD'S PROMISE TO YOU I am the LORD, and I do not change. MALACHI 3:6

God, how can I live in today's culture without compromising my convictions?

ANSWER FROM GOD'S WORD Don't copy the behavior and customs of this world, but let God transform you into a new person by changing the way you think. Then you will learn to know God's will for you, which is good and pleasing and perfect. ROMANS 12:2

Popular culture exerts enormous pressure to shape your life, pressuring you to conform and fit in, and challenging what you believe. Without even realizing it, you may be copying lifestyle choices that are cultural rather than biblical. To follow God's will, you must first be familiar with his Word. Transformation happens when God's Word informs your worldview and changes the way you think about and respond to culture.

GOD'S PROMISE TO YOU Joyful are those who obey his laws and search for him with all their hearts. They do not compromise with evil, and they walk only in his paths. PSALM 119:2-3

God, what can I do if I start to lose confidence in you?

ANSWER FROM GOD'S WORD The LORD is my light and my salvation—so why should I be afraid? The LORD is my fortress, protecting me from danger, so why should I tremble? PSALM 27:1

Your confidence comes not from your physical circumstances (how you look or what you achieve), but from the inner assurance that God is by your side, making his wisdom and power available to you and working out his purpose for your life. If you begin to lose confidence in God, go to his promises in the Bible. Remember the promises he has already fulfilled and take comfort from those. Your confidence in him will be restored.

GOD'S PROMISE TO YOU His faithful promises are your armor and protection. PSALM 91:4

God, where can I find courage to do the right thing, or to go on when life seems too hard?

ANSWER FROM GOD'S WORD This is my command—be strong and courageous! Do not be afraid or discouraged. For the LORD your God is with you wherever you go. JOSHUA 1:9

True courage comes from understanding that God is stronger than your biggest problem or your worst enemy and that he wants to use his power to help you. Courage is not misplaced confidence in your own strength; it is well-placed confidence in God's strength. Fear comes from feeling alone against a great threat. Courage comes from knowing that God is beside you, helping you fight the threat. To stay courageous, focus more on God's power and less on your problem.

GOD'S PROMISE TO YOU The LORD your God . . . is with you! DEUTERONOMY 20:1

God, are demons and spiritual warfare real?

ANSWER FROM GOD'S WORD We are not fighting against flesh-and-blood enemies, but against evil rulers and authorities of the unseen world, against mighty powers in this dark world, and against evil spirits in the heavenly places.
EPHESIANS 6:12

There is a real spiritual battle raging all around us. Although we cannot see it, we can see the results manifested in evil acts and broken lives. Demons are very real and are on the attack. Motivated by Satan, their intentions are to harm, to destroy, and to turn people away from obeying God. The good news is that God is so much more powerful than Satan or any demon, and they are ultimately subject to his authority. Demons, as fallen angels, have limited power, and the Bible describes them as cowering before God in fear. Therefore, if you believe in God and his mighty power, you can rely on that power to be victorious in your spiritual battles and to resist temptation.

GOD'S PROMISE TO YOU The Lord is faithful; he will strengthen you and guard you from the evil one. 2 THESSALONIANS 3:3

God, what does it mean to depend on you?

ANSWER FROM GOD'S WORD O our God, we thank you and praise your glorious name! But who am I, and who are my people, that we could give anything to you? Everything we have has come from you, and we give you only what you first gave us! 1 CHRONICLES 29:13-14

Depending on God means recognizing him as the source of your strength, your successes, and all good things in your life. Everything you have ultimately comes from his hand. Because he created you, he knows you inside and out, so you can depend on him to guide you into what is best for you. Dependence on God, your Provider, brings you peace, knowing that you will have everything you need.

GOD'S PROMISE TO YOU Deep in your hearts you know that every promise of the LORD your God has come true. Not a single one has failed! JOSHUA 23:14

God, do I really have a destiny?

ANSWER FROM GOD'S WORD You guide me with your counsel, leading me to a glorious destiny. PSALM 73:24

It is your destiny to one day live with God in his eternal Kingdom. When you pursue this goal first and embrace it with your whole heart, you will live your life to the fullest with absolute confidence that you are fulfilling your destiny on earth. This confidence will give you purpose and hope as you persevere through the troubles of life.

GOD'S PROMISE TO YOU That is what God is like. He is our God forever and ever, and he will guide us until we die. PSALM 48:14

God, how can I keep discovering new things about you?

ANSWER FROM GOD'S WORD I will pursue your commands, for you expand my understanding. PSALM 119:32

One of the best ways to discover more about God is to read his Word. The Bible is filled with accounts of God's actions throughout history, his concern for individuals and groups of people, his plans for creation, his promises, and his commands. Throughout the Bible, God demonstrates his character, unveils his redemptive plan, and reveals truth. Because God is infinite, there is no limit to what you can discover about him. The more you desire to know him, the more you will want to keep pursuing him.

GOD'S PROMISE TO YOU I will give you treasures hidden in the darkness—secret riches. I will do this so you may know that I am the LORD, . . . the one who calls you by name. ISAIAH 45:3

God, when I have doubts, does it mean my faith isn't real?

ANSWER FROM GOD'S WORD John the Baptist . . . sent his disciples to ask Jesus, "Are you the Messiah we've been expecting, or should we keep looking for someone else?" MATTHEW 11:2-3

Many "pillars of faith" in the Bible had moments of doubt. Doubt does not necessarily indicate a lack of faith. In fact, it may signal a deeper embracing of faith. Life doesn't always make sense; we wrestle with questions such as *Why does evil seem to prosper? Why do good people sometimes die young? Why do children have to suffer?* Tough issues like these may challenge your faith. But don't let doubt drive you away from God. Instead, use your doubt as motivation to get to know God even better. Let doubt initiate a new conversation with God, to help you make more sense of what confuses you. God welcomes your doubt as an opportunity to give you new insights about how to love him and others in the chaos of a fallen world.

GOD'S PROMISE TO YOU God has said, "I will never fail you. I will never abandon you." HEBREWS 13:5

God, how do you encourage me when I feel down?

ANSWER FROM GOD'S WORD May our Lord Jesus Christ himself and God our Father, who loved us and by his grace gave us eternal comfort and a wonderful hope, comfort you and strengthen you in every good thing you do and say. 2 THESSALONIANS 2:16-17

When your world seems to be crashing down around you and nothing is going well, it's comforting to know that your heavenly Father already knows exactly what you need. He knows whether your discouragement is from physical weariness, emotional strain, mental taxation, or relational strife, and he is ready to meet you at your point of need. He will encourage you through his Word with comfort, hope, and strength. Turn to him every day and bask in his love.

GOD'S PROMISE TO YOU The humble will see their God at work and be glad. Let all who seek God's help be encouraged. PSALM 69:32

God, will eternity in heaven be boring?

ANSWER FROM GOD'S WORD God has made everything beautiful for its own time. He has planted eternity in the human heart.
ECCLESIASTES 3:11

King Solomon wrote that God has planted eternity in the human heart. This means that we innately know there is more than just this life. God has built into our hearts a restless yearning for the kind of perfect world that can be found only in heaven. Through nature, art, and relationships, he gives us a glimpse of that world. Someday he will restore the earth to the way it was when he first created it, when it was perfect. Eternity will be a never-ending exploration of its beauty and a perfect relationship with God.

GOD'S PROMISE TO YOU Look! I am creating new heavens and a new earth, and no one will even think about the old ones anymore. Be glad; rejoice forever in my creation! ISAIAH 65:17-18

God, how should my faith in you affect the way I live?

ANSWER FROM GOD'S WORD Faith shows the reality of what we hope for; it is the evidence of things we cannot see. HEBREWS 11:1

Faith is more than simply believing something; it is living your life according to what you believe. It is confident conviction, not wishful thinking. Faith in God means that you pattern your life after the principles in the Bible because you trust that God's ways are best. When faced with decisions, you make choices based on God's Word, confident that all his promises will come true. Faith encourages choices today that will have an impact for eternity. Instead of living for yourself, you live in a way that serves others and pleases the Lord.

GOD'S PROMISE TO YOU I tell you the truth, those who listen to my message and believe in God who sent me have eternal life. JOHN 5:24

God, what does it mean to fear you?

ANSWER FROM GOD'S WORD Fear of the LORD is the foundation of wisdom. Knowledge of the Holy One results in good judgment.
PROVERBS 9:10

Fearing God is not the same as being afraid of him. Being afraid of someone drives you away. Fearing God means being awed by his power and goodness—which should draw you closer to him and to the blessings he gives. When you fear God, it is similar to having respect for a beloved teacher, coach, parent, or mentor who motivates you to do your best. You naturally want to avoid doing anything that would offend that person or provoke his or her displeasure. You fear God because of his awesome power; you love God for his goodness, shown in the ways he helps you, loves you, and blesses you.

GOD'S PROMISE TO YOU Serve the LORD with reverent fear, and rejoice with trembling.
PSALM 2:11

God, can studying the Bible really make a difference in my life?

ANSWER FROM GOD'S WORD Study this Book of Instruction continually. Meditate on it day and night so you will be sure to obey everything written in it. Only then will you prosper and succeed in all you do. JOSHUA 1:8

Because God's wisdom is infinite, his Word shapes our character and guides us through life, speaking into every relationship and circumstance. When we study God's Word, we gain a deeper understanding of who God is and who we are, making it easier for us to recognize truth and gain a greater awareness of how we can love God and follow him wholeheartedly. His Word guides us as we grow into spiritual maturity. Bible study is an important discipline as it aligns our worldview with God's.

GOD'S PROMISE TO YOU The instructions of the LORD are perfect, reviving the soul. The decrees of the LORD are trustworthy, making wise the simple. PSALM 19:7

God, why does following you seem so hard sometimes?

ANSWER FROM GOD'S WORD If any of you wants to be my follower, you must give up your own way, take up your cross, and follow me. MATTHEW 16:24

No one follows God because it's easy. We follow God because what he says is true, right, and good. Living his way brings us purpose and fulfillment, peace of mind, and an understanding of real love. The right way is often harder than the easy way, but it's so much better. God says that only *his* way is true. If you do not follow what is true, you will follow what is false or counterfeit, leading to confusion, sin, and separation from God. When God leads you in a certain direction, don't give up just because the going gets tough. Keep moving forward with your eyes fixed on him. Your faith will be strengthened as you obey him.

GOD'S PROMISE TO YOU When troubles of any kind come your way, consider it an opportunity for great joy. For you know that when your faith is tested, your endurance has a chance to grow. So let it grow, for when your endurance is fully developed, you will be perfect and complete, needing nothing. JAMES 1:2-4

God, how can I be a good person?

ANSWER FROM GOD'S WORD Make every effort to respond to God's promises. Supplement your faith with a generous provision of moral excellence, and moral excellence with knowledge, and knowledge with self-control, and self-control with patient endurance, and patient endurance with godliness, and godliness with brotherly affection, and brotherly affection with love for everyone. 2 PETER 1:5-7

True goodness runs deeper than nice actions; it reflects a heart of integrity. If you want to be a good person, you must be willing for God to change you inside, deep down in the inner core. As you become more and more like Jesus, your actions will reflect his goodness. As he takes control of your heart, you will begin doing good deeds, which when practiced over a lifetime will result in the character quality of *goodness*.

GOD'S PROMISE TO YOU This is what the LORD says: "Stop at the crossroads and look around. Ask for the old, godly way, and walk in it. Travel its path, and you will find rest for your souls." JEREMIAH 6:16

God, how does grace affect the way I live?

God saved you by his grace when you believed. And you can't take credit for this; it is a gift from God. EPHESIANS 2:8

Grace is a beautiful gift that reveals the compassionate heart of God. Grace is God's gift, not the product of your own effort. This gives you permission to live in the freedom of God's grace, rather than wallowing in guilt. When you grasp the wonderful concept that God loves you and has broken the power of sin through Jesus' death on the cross, you will experience the transforming power of God's grace in your life.

GOD'S PROMISE TO YOU Sin is no longer your master, for you no longer live under the requirements of the law. Instead, you live under the freedom of God's grace. ROMANS 6:14

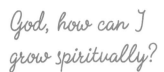

God, how can I grow spiritually?

ANSWER FROM GOD'S WORD Let us stop going over the basic teachings about Christ again and again. Let us go on instead and become mature in our understanding. . . . Let your roots grow down into him, and let your lives be built on him. Then your faith will grow strong in the truth you were taught. HEBREWS 6:1; COLOSSIANS 2:7

Spiritual growth is like physical growth: You start small and grow one day at a time. In order to grow, however, you need nourishment. Spiritually, you are fed by challenging your mind with the study of God's Word, asking questions about it, and finding answers through prayer and the counsel of other believers. Look at each day as a building block. When you commit yourself to building a life of godly character one day at a time, you will find yourself becoming spiritually mature.

GOD'S PROMISE TO YOU Christ will make his home in your hearts as you trust in him. Your roots will grow down into God's love and keep you strong. EPHESIANS 3:17

God, is Jesus the only way to heaven?

ANSWER FROM GOD'S WORD Jesus told him, "I am the way, the truth, and the life. No one can come to the Father except through me."
JOHN 14:6

Many people assume if they live good lives they will go to heaven. Many other faiths are based on merit, earning one's way to heaven through good deeds. Though a person may lead a wonderful life, it is not the way that leads to eternal life with God in heaven. Even a good life, if lived apart from God, isn't enough to bridge the gap between this world and the new world God will establish at the end of history. Jesus is that bridge. There is just the one way, and it's open to anyone who chooses to follow it.

GOD'S PROMISE TO YOU If you openly declare that Jesus is Lord and believe in your heart that God raised him from the dead, you will be saved.
ROMANS 10:9

God, what does it mean to be holy?

ANSWER FROM GOD'S WORD You were cleansed; you were made holy; you were made right with God by calling on the name of the Lord Jesus Christ and by the Spirit of our God.
1 CORINTHIANS 6:11

God makes you holy by forgiving your sins. When you belong to Jesus, God looks at you as if you had never sinned. But though he sees you as holy, you are not yet perfected in holiness. Each day, God leads you by faith to work out your salvation and to grow in holiness as you become more like Jesus. You try to live each day dedicated and devoted to God and his way of living, which makes your life distinct and set apart from the way most of the world chooses to live.

GOD'S PROMISE TO YOU Even before he made the world, God loved us and chose us in Christ to be holy and without fault in his eyes.
EPHESIANS 1:4

God, how can I become more hopeful?

Such things were written in the Scriptures long ago to teach us. And the Scriptures give us hope and encouragement as we wait patiently for God's promises to be fulfilled. ROMANS 15:4

Hope can be cultivated by reading God's Word. Its stories and promises remind you of God's miraculous love and plan for his people. As you see how God's hand has worked in the lives of his people throughout history, you will find yourself gaining hope and confidence that he will work in your life as well because you are one of his. Each day let God's Word renew your hope in a fresh way, specific to your needs. As you review his promises for your future, you will find yourself anticipating how God will work each day. In the darkest of times, God's Word will lift you up.

GOD'S PROMISE TO YOU O Lord, you alone are my hope. PSALM 71:5

God, how can I know if my life is counting for Jesus?

ANSWER FROM GOD'S WORD We are only God's servants through whom you believed the Good News. Each of us did the work the Lord gave us. I planted the seed in your hearts, and Apollos watered it, but it was God who made it grow. 1 CORINTHIANS 3:5-6

This side of eternity, you may not always be able to see how your life affects others. You may be planting seeds of faith in the lives of people around you, and those seeds will grow into faith you will never even know about. Instead of trying to make an impact, live every day in obedience to God. Years of life built on daily obedience develop the character and integrity that draw others to Jesus.

GOD'S PROMISE TO YOU The one who plants and the one who waters work together with the same purpose. And both will be rewarded for their own hard work. 1 CORINTHIANS 3:8

God, how do you transform my life?

ANSWER FROM GOD'S WORD The kind of sorrow God wants us to experience leads us away from sin and results in salvation. There's no regret for that kind of sorrow. 2 CORINTHIANS 7:10

Sometimes God initiates a change of heart in you so that you desire to have a deeper relationship with him. Sometimes God reveals sin in your heart so you will change your course. When God convicts you of wrongful ways, he also guides you back to the right path. He will never initiate a change of heart and then abandon you. God desires that you be a part of his work, and he will be with you, molding you into the kind of person he can use.

GOD'S PROMISE TO YOU Since our friendship with God was restored by the death of his Son while we were still his enemies, we will certainly be saved through the life of his Son. ROMANS 5:10

God, how can I find more meaning in my life?

ANSWER FROM GOD'S WORD Tune your ears to wisdom, and concentrate on understanding. Cry out for insight, and ask for understanding. Search for them as you would for silver; seek them like hidden treasures. PROVERBS 2:2-4

Only God's purpose for you will satisfy you, because he created you specifically for that purpose. Because he is the creator of life, only he can teach you how to live your life in a meaningful way. So, dig into God's Word and pursue him in prayer, asking him to reveal his truth to you and to fulfill his purpose in you. You will discover God's plans for your life as you diligently do this. He will not fail to use you for his purpose if you are surrendered to his ways. Pursuit of anything else will leave you empty.

GOD'S PROMISE TO YOU The thief's purpose is to steal and kill and destroy. My purpose is to give them a rich and satisfying life. JOHN 10:10

God, why do I need your mercy?

ANSWER FROM GOD'S WORD The LORD is compassionate and merciful, slow to get angry and filled with unfailing love. He will not constantly accuse us, nor remain angry forever. He does not punish us for all our sins; he does not deal harshly with us, as we deserve. PSALM 103:8-10

Mercy is more than exemption from the punishment of sin. It is an undeserved gift—salvation from eternal death, and life forever with God in heaven. God's mercies never end. He never stops giving you his undivided attention, faithful presence, spiritual gifts, provision for your needs, and hope for your future—all undeserved and yet lavishly poured out in your life. It is by his mercies that your very life is sustained.

GOD'S PROMISE TO YOU The faithful love of the LORD never ends! His mercies never cease. Great is his faithfulness; his mercies begin afresh each morning. LAMENTATIONS 3:22-23

God, do you still perform miracles today?

ANSWER FROM GOD'S WORD Come and see what our God has done, what awesome miracles he performs for people! PSALM 66:5

You have a miracle-working God who is able—and willing—to do the impossible for you. Consider these small miracles that happen in life: a breathtaking sunset; the restoration of a broken relationship; the birth of a baby; the healing of an illness; the rebirth of the earth in spring; salvation by faith in Jesus alone; the work of love and forgiveness that changes someone's life; hearing the specific call of God in your life. If you think you've never seen a miracle, look closer. With the confidence that God is working miracles all around you, you can better anticipate the even bigger miracles he wants to do for you!

GOD'S PROMISE TO YOU No pagan god is like you, O Lord. None can do what you do! PSALM 86:8

God, why don't you make everything clearer?

ANSWER FROM GOD'S WORD Just as you cannot understand the path of the wind or the mystery of a tiny baby growing in its mother's womb, so you cannot understand the activity of God, who does all things. ECCLESIASTES 11:5

God's mysteries are opportunities for faith. If you knew everything about God or his plans for your life, there would be no need for faith. God has given you all you need to know to believe in him. Don't be discouraged by the mysteries of God. Instead, remind yourself what he has already revealed about himself to you. You are not responsible for what you can't know about God, but you are responsible to use what you do know to obey and worship him and to serve others.

GOD'S PROMISE TO YOU By his divine power, God has given us everything we need for living a godly life. We have received all of this by coming to know him, the one who called us to himself by means of his marvelous glory and excellence. 2 PETER 1:3

God, how can I know if my motives are pure?

ANSWER FROM GOD'S WORD Put me on trial, LORD, and cross-examine me. Test my motives and my heart. PSALM 26:2

God challenges you to examine your heart; that is, to test your motives to discover what you value most. Ask yourself these "heart test" questions: (1) How do you respond when God asks you to give up something to follow him? (2) Would you do something God asked of you even if everyone else thought it was crazy? (3) Where do you spend your money, and what does that reveal about your values? The Lord knows your heart, but he wants you to be aware of your motives too.

GOD'S PROMISE TO YOU I will give you a new heart, and I will put a new spirit in you. I will take out your stony, stubborn heart and give you a tender, responsive heart. EZEKIEL 36:26

God, how can I know you listen when I pray?

ANSWER FROM GOD'S WORD The eyes of the LORD watch over those who do right, and his ears are open to their prayers. 1 PETER 3:12

God loves you enough to listen, like an attentive parent who bends down to hear what his child is saying. God hears your prayers for forgiveness and your cries for help. You are God's precious child, and he is always listening. That doesn't mean God gives you whatever you ask for; no loving parent would do that. But he promises that every prayer will be heard and answered in the way that is best for you and that fulfills his greatest purpose for you.

GOD'S PROMISE TO YOU As soon as I pray, you answer me; you encourage me by giving me strength. PSALM 138:3

God, what does it mean to love my neighbor?

ANSWER FROM GOD'S WORD "Which of these three would you say was a neighbor to the man who was attacked by bandits?" Jesus asked. The man replied, "The one who showed him mercy." Then Jesus said, "Yes, now go and do the same." LUKE 10:36-37

Jesus' teachings expand your "neighborhood" to include anyone around you who is in need—in need of love, comfort, help, friendship, or encouragement. This means that your coworkers, the person next to you on the plane, and the homeless people in your town are also your neighbors. When you begin to view people you see, meet, or even hear about as your neighbors, you will begin to see encounters with them as opportunities to share the love of Jesus by offering a helping hand. What neighbors have crossed your path today?

GOD'S PROMISE TO YOU It is good when you obey the royal law as found in the Scriptures: "Love your neighbor as yourself." JAMES 2:8

God, why do you pursue a relationship with me?

ANSWER FROM GOD'S WORD Surely your goodness and unfailing love will pursue me all the days of my life, and I will live in the house of the LORD forever. PSALM 23:6

God is looking for a personal relationship with each person he created. He pursues you not to get something from you but to give you something wonderful: help, hope, power, salvation, joy, peace, and eternal life. He pursues you because he knows these gifts can transform your life. God wants to shower his abundant love on you because you are precious to him.

GOD'S PROMISE TO YOU I have loved you, my people, with an everlasting love. With unfailing love I have drawn you to myself. JEREMIAH 31:3

God, do I need a spiritual mentor?

ANSWER FROM GOD'S WORD When they came to the other side, Elijah said to Elisha, "Tell me what I can do for you before I am taken away." And Elisha replied, "Please let me inherit a double share of your spirit and become your successor." 2 KINGS 2:9

Other people can inspire passion for God in you. A godly mentor, teacher, or friend can open your eyes to the wonderful blessings of serving God and walking in his ways. Elijah was Elisha's mentor. As Elisha watched and learned from the great prophet, he was inspired to become Elijah's successor and an even greater prophet. Likewise, your walk with God can inspire others to pursue God and serve him even more passionately.

GOD'S PROMISE TO YOU Those who listen to instruction will prosper; those who trust the LORD will be joyful. PROVERBS 16:20

God, how can I find peace?

ANSWER FROM GOD'S WORD Don't worry about anything; instead, pray about everything. Tell God what you need, and thank him for all he has done. Then you will experience God's peace, which exceeds anything we can understand. His peace will guard your hearts and minds as you live in Christ Jesus. PHILIPPIANS 4:6-7

When life starts to spin out of control, prayer can become your gateway to peace. Your spirit will lighten as you unburden your soul to God. His peace is like a guard on patrol, protecting you from assaults of anxiety or concern. Your problems will always control you when you focus solely on them. Focusing on God's goodness and his promises helps you see the resources available to you from the Lord. Then you can experience peace despite your problems.

GOD'S PROMISE TO YOU You will keep in perfect peace all who trust in you, all whose thoughts are fixed on you! ISAIAH 26:3

God, how do I experience more of your power in my life?

ANSWER FROM GOD'S WORD This is the secret: Christ lives in you. This gives you assurance of sharing his glory. . . . That's why I work and struggle so hard, depending on Christ's mighty power that works within me. COLOSSIANS 1:27, 29

The secret to experiencing God's power is first to realize that his power is available to you. When you believe in Jesus, God's very Spirit comes to live in you. Then, no matter what you face in life, you don't have to rely on your own strength; you can rely on God's. His power is most evident in your weaknesses and vulnerabilities, because then you know that only by his strength are you able to accomplish what you cannot do on your own. When opposition or problems arise, try not to look at the size of the problem but at the size of your God. When there are great things to be done, you have a great God who is able to do them through you.

GOD'S PROMISE TO YOU The LORD is my strength and my song; he has given me victory. PSALM 118:14

God, how can I become passionate about the same things you care about?

ANSWER FROM GOD'S WORD God knows how often I pray for you. Day and night I bring you and your needs in prayer to God, whom I serve with all my heart by spreading the Good News about his Son. ROMANS 1:9

God often reveals his desires for your life when you are praying to him. As you talk with God and align your mind with his, his desires become yours as well. Praying Scripture can give words to your emotions. Try reading through the Psalms and praying God's Word back to him. His Word is often the language the Holy Spirit uses to speak inspiration to your heart. When you pray in line with God's Word, you become passionate about his desires.

GOD'S PROMISE TO YOU Take delight in the LORD, and he will give you your heart's desires. PSALM 37:4

God, will you get angry if I question your plan for my life?

ANSWER FROM GOD'S WORD I will climb up to my watchtower and stand at my guardpost. There I will wait to see what the LORD says and how he will answer my complaint. HABAKKUK 2:1

God is patient when you question his plans for your life. He welcomes your questions, but most often he reveals his faithful character rather than specific plans for your future. God encourages tough questions because it is in the questions that your relationship with him grows as you learn to trust that his plans for you are good. God's greatest plan for you is to know him and love him. As this happens, you will become less concerned about specific plans for your future and more interested in his plan to transform you into his likeness. Then you will experience purpose and joy in whatever you do.

GOD'S PROMISE TO YOU If you need wisdom, ask our generous God, and he will give it to you. He will not rebuke you for asking. JAMES 1:5

God, how should I relate to those less fortunate?

ANSWER FROM GOD'S WORD When you harvest the crops of your land, do not harvest the grain along the edges of your fields. . . . Leave [it] for the poor and the foreigners living among you. LEVITICUS 19:9-10

God has compassion for those in need, so godliness should include a deep compassion for others. Throughout the Bible, God demonstrates his daily care for the poor. In these verses from Leviticus 19, he instructs farmers to leave some grain and fruit in their fields after harvest so those in need can find food. What can you give from your abundance? Helping the poor and needy is not merely an obligation; it is a privilege that brings great joy and blessing from God.

GOD'S PROMISE TO YOU If you help the poor, you are lending to the LORD—and he will repay you! PROVERBS 19:17

God, can I approach you with my problems?

ANSWER FROM GOD'S WORD This High Priest of ours understands our weaknesses, for he faced all of the same testings we do, yet he did not sin. So let us come boldly to the throne of our gracious God. There we will receive his mercy, and we will find grace to help us when we need it most. HEBREWS 4:15-16

God will never say, "Sorry, I don't have time for you" or "I'm busy." He understands your weak moments because Jesus himself experienced the difficulties of life. He always listens, always responds, and always loves. Even at your weakest, he does not reject you but rather embraces you, so that you can receive strength to be all he intends you to be.

GOD'S PROMISE TO YOU Because of Christ and our faith in him, we can now come boldly and confidently into God's presence. EPHESIANS 3:12

God, when you are silent, does that mean you've rejected me?

ANSWER FROM GOD'S WORD Tell me, what have I done wrong? Show me my rebellion and my sin. Why do you turn away from me? Why do you treat me as your enemy? JOB 13:23-24

Don't misinterpret God's silence as rejection. He promises never to reject those who love him. He might be quiet so that you will draw closer to him to hear him more fully and experience his love and acceptance. Sometimes God is silent because he is waiting to reveal something to you at the proper time. In times when God seems silent, trust his loving character and his promise never to abandon you.

GOD'S PROMISE TO YOU The LORD will not reject his people; he will not abandon his special possession. PSALM 94:14

God, how are you present in my relationships with others?

ANSWER FROM GOD'S WORD   Jesus replied, "'You must love the LORD your God with all your heart, all your soul, and all your mind.' This is the first and greatest commandment. A second is equally important: 'Love your neighbor as yourself.'"   MATTHEW 22:37-39

It is often through our relationships that we learn more about relating to God. Likewise, as you deepen your relationship with God, you will also learn more about relating to others. God knows how important relationships are, so he has given you the tools and his own Holy Spirit to help you relate effectively to others. Your relationships are opportunities to respond with gratitude for God's faithfulness to you. When you love others, you reflect the love God has for you.

GOD'S PROMISE TO YOU   Now we can rejoice in our wonderful new relationship with God because our Lord Jesus Christ has made us friends of God. ROMANS 5:11

God, can you renew my life?

ANSWER FROM GOD'S WORD Put on your new nature, and be renewed as you learn to know your Creator and become like him. COLOSSIANS 3:10

Sometimes the routine of life can leave us feeling burned out and exhausted. We long for a new approach to life but may not know how to get there. You always have a chance for a fresh start with God. Begin by admitting what isn't working in your life, the sinful habits that hold you back, and your desire to start anew. As you learn to know God and his Word more and more, his Spirit will renew your thoughts and actions and give you a fresh approach to life.

GOD'S PROMISE TO YOU My health may fail, and my spirit may grow weak, but God remains the strength of my heart; he is mine forever. PSALM 73:26

God, how can turning away from my sin change my life?

ANSWER FROM GOD'S WORD Finally, I confessed all my sins to you and stopped trying to hide my guilt. I said to myself, "I will confess my rebellion to the LORD." And you forgave me! All my guilt is gone. PSALM 32:5

Repentance begins with confession—being humbly honest with God and being sincerely sorry for your sins. God removes your guilt, restores your joy, and starts the process of restoration and transformation. A heart that truly longs for change is necessary for repentance to be genuine. When God forgives your sins, your life journey takes a new direction, following God's life-giving path.

GOD'S PROMISE TO YOU There is joy in the presence of God's angels when even one sinner repents. LUKE 15:10

God, what does sacred mean? Is my life sacred?

ANSWER FROM GOD'S WORD Don't you realize that your body is the temple of the Holy Spirit, who lives in you and was given to you by God?
1 CORINTHIANS 6:19

Sacred means "set apart for God" or "dedicated to the purposes of God." When objects are deemed sacred, they are regarded with respect and honor. You are set apart for God. Even more, your body is the very dwelling place of God's Holy Spirit. When you sincerely try to avoid sin and dedicate yourself to following God wholeheartedly, your life becomes sacred—set apart as special to him and ready to fulfill all the wonderful things he has planned for you.

GOD'S PROMISE TO YOU Now may the God of peace make you holy in every way, and may your whole spirit and soul and body be kept blameless until our Lord Jesus Christ comes again.
1 THESSALONIANS 5:23

God, how does salvation affect my daily life?

ANSWER FROM GOD'S WORD We are God's masterpiece. He has created us anew in Christ Jesus, so we can do the good things he planned for us long ago. EPHESIANS 2:10

Salvation happens the moment you accept Jesus Christ as your Savior. This, of course, secures your eternal future, but it also infuses your daily life with joy, peace, hope, divine wisdom, and a deeper love for others. You can live every single day with an eternal perspective, which helps you see that this world is not all there is. Salvation is also a process; God is working in you each day, growing you toward spiritual maturity and deeper faith in him. In every season, he has good things planned for you, giving you a sense each day of his purpose for you.

GOD'S PROMISE TO YOU Since we have been made right in God's sight by faith, we have peace with God because of what Jesus Christ our Lord has done for us. ROMANS 5:1

God, how can I overcome spiritual blindness?

ANSWER FROM GOD'S WORD Sin whispers to the wicked, deep within their hearts. They have no fear of God at all. In their blind conceit, they cannot see how wicked they really are. PSALM 36:1-2

Spiritual blindness means being unaware of your need for God and living without acknowledging him. This way of living can lead to pride and self-centeredness, diminishing your ability to perceive truth. Spiritual vision is connected to a humble heart. When you recognize that your own way is not best and that you need divine help, God opens your spiritual eyes to his ways, lights the proper path ahead of you, and guides you as you trust his direction for your life.

GOD'S PROMISE TO YOU Jesus told him, "I entered this world to render judgment—to give sight to the blind and to show those who think they see that they are blind." JOHN 9:39

God, do I really need to be involved at church?

ANSWER FROM GOD'S WORD Just as our bodies have many parts and each part has a special function, so it is with Christ's body. We are many parts of one body, and we all belong to each other. ROMANS 12:4-5

God has given every believer special gifts. Some people are great organizers or administrators; others are gifted musicians, teachers, or evangelists. When the members of a congregation use their gifts to serve, the church becomes a powerful force for good, a strong witness for Jesus, and a mighty army to combat Satan's attacks against God's people. The church needs you because the body of Christ is not complete unless you are there and active.

GOD'S PROMISE TO YOU All of you together are Christ's body, and each of you is a part of it. 1 CORINTHIANS 12:27

God, what is the benefit of surrendering my life to you?

ANSWER FROM GOD'S WORD What do you benefit if you gain the whole world but are yourself lost or destroyed? LUKE 9:25

When you surrender your life to God, you are not left empty. Surrendering your life doesn't mean not having a life. In fact, God gives you a new life far better than your old one. He fills your heart with joy and replaces your old sinful desires with new and better desires. Surrendering to God allows you to receive his abundance. You receive this new and better way of life only by giving up your old one. When you surrender your life here on earth to God, he gives you eternal life in exchange.

GOD'S PROMISE TO YOU If you try to hang on to your life, you will lose it. But if you give up your life for my sake, you will save it. MATTHEW 16:25

God, why should I practice gratitude?

ANSWER FROM GOD'S WORD Be thankful in all circumstances, for this is God's will for you who belong to Christ Jesus. 1 THESSALONIANS 5:18

The blessing of a spirit of gratitude is a new outlook on life. Thankfulness changes the way you look at your circumstances. Complaining connects you to unhappiness—gratitude and praise connect you to the source of real joy. When you make thanksgiving a regular part of your life, you stay focused on what God has done and continues to do for you. Expressing gratitude for God's help and blessings is a form of worship. When you give thanks to God, you honor and praise him for what he has done in your life.

GOD'S PROMISE TO YOU Giving thanks is a sacrifice that truly honors me. If you keep to my path, I will reveal to you the salvation of God. PSALM 50:23

God, how can trusting your plan for my future help me live today?

ANSWER FROM GOD'S WORD The Lord says, "I will guide you along the best pathway for your life. I will advise you and watch over you." PSALM 32:8

God's promise to guide you is life-changing. You can discover and take part in the plan God has for you, knowing it is the best pathway for your life. You can be confident that nothing can harm your soul or your eternal future. You can take risks and walk in faith when God asks you to do something for him. You can be generous and experience peace of mind. You can live knowing that your future will be everything God planned for you.

GOD'S PROMISE TO YOU Because we are united with Christ, we have received an inheritance from God, for he chose us in advance, and he makes everything work out according to his plan. EPHESIANS 1:11

God, how can I make the most of the time I have?

ANSWER FROM GOD'S WORD Teach us to realize the brevity of life, so that we may grow in wisdom. PSALM 90:12

How you use your time on earth will affect your life in heaven. God does not ask you to do everything, just everything he has called you to do—and he assures you that there is time for whatever it is. The more you invest in discovering the purpose for which God created you and how to live out that purpose with obedience and responsibility, the more significant your time on earth will become.

GOD'S PROMISE TO YOU Those who are wise will find a time and a way to do what is right, for there is a time and a way for everything, even when a person is in trouble. ECCLESIASTES 8:5-6

God, how do you refresh me in times of stress?

ANSWER FROM GOD'S WORD Jesus said, "Come to me, all of you who are weary and carry heavy burdens, and I will give you rest." MATTHEW 11:28

Here are some ways God will renew your strength when you grow weary. When you come to him in praise, he refreshes your heart. When you come to him in prayer, he refreshes your soul. When you come to him in meditation, he refreshes your mind. When you come to him in solitude, he refreshes your body. When you come to him with thankfulness, he refreshes your perspective. Practicing these disciplines helps you release the burdens of life and draw new energy from God, the source of your strength.

GOD'S PROMISE TO YOU I lay down and slept, yet I woke up in safety, for the LORD was watching over me. PSALM 3:5

God, why don't you answer my prayers right away?

ANSWER FROM GOD'S WORD The LORD is good to those who depend on him, to those who search for him. So it is good to wait quietly for salvation from the LORD. And it is good for people to submit at an early age to the yoke of his discipline. LAMENTATIONS 3:25-27

Sometimes waiting is best for you. God often leads you on the path of progressive victory instead of immediate victory, for the sake of your own personal growth. God knows that if you got everything you wanted or needed right away, you would not rely on him as much and you would not grow in character or maturity. Stress builds strength. As you wait for God to act, serve him where you are and make the most of the adversities that come your way. God will act when the timing is best for you.

GOD'S PROMISE TO YOU Those who trust in the LORD will find new strength. They will soar high on wings like eagles. They will run and not grow weary. They will walk and not faint. ISAIAH 40:31

God, why is worshiping you important?

ANSWER FROM GOD'S WORD Let us worship and bow down. Let us kneel before the LORD our maker, for he is our God. We are the people he watches over, the flock under his care. If only you would listen to his voice today! PSALM 95:6-7

Worship is the recognition of who God is and of who you are in relation to him. Ultimately, everything you do should be based on what you think of God and how you worship him. If your actions don't pay homage to him, then you are paying homage to someone or something else. Human beings were created to worship—to ascribe value to something or someone—and to prioritize our lives accordingly. The Bible teaches that God alone is worthy of your ultimate worship. When you take time to praise God whenever you see his wisdom, power, direction, care, and love in your life, you are honoring him. Worship then becomes a way of life, deepening your relationship with God and strengthening your ability to communicate with him.

GOD'S PROMISE TO YOU Everything on earth will worship you; they will sing your praises, shouting your name in glorious songs. PSALM 66:4

God, how can I become more like Jesus every day?

ANSWER FROM GOD'S WORD Even the Son of Man came not to be served but to serve others and to give his life as a ransom for many.
MARK 10:45

Jesus glorified God in everything he did. His focus on his Father shaped the way he lived every day, helping him to serve others in every interaction while faithfully obeying the truths of God's Word. As you face each day, ask yourself these questions: *Will my plans for today please God? How can I love or serve those with whom I interact today? How would Jesus face the challenges I'll face today?* These questions will help guide your thoughts and actions, giving you vision for how to spend the day. Then, day by day, God will help you grow to become more like Jesus.

GOD'S PROMISE TO YOU We will speak the truth in love, growing in every way more and more like Christ, who is the head of his body, the church. EPHESIANS 4:15

God, how can I discover where my gifts can best be used?

ANSWER FROM GOD'S WORD There are different kinds of spiritual gifts, but the same Spirit is the source of them all. There are different kinds of service, but we serve the same Lord. God works in different ways, but it is the same God who does the work in all of us. 1 CORINTHIANS 12:4-6

The natural abilities you have are gifts from God, and they are often a clue to what God wants you to do. You may have natural gifts for cooking, entertaining, managing a business, teaching, handling money, playing an instrument, or any number of other things. Use whatever gifts you possess to serve others and glorify God. It is often through trying new things and serving that we discover our gifts and how best to use them.

GOD'S PROMISE TO YOU In his grace, God has given us different gifts for doing certain things well. ROMANS 12:6

God, do you care about the little details of my life?

ANSWER FROM GOD'S WORD The LORD directs the steps of the godly. He delights in every detail of their lives. PSALM 37:23

When you are faced with a decision or a problem, you may be afraid to bother God because you think he has bigger things to worry about. But nothing could be further from the truth. God wants to help you because he loves you. He cares about your little decisions as much as your big ones. God invites you to share your small cares as well as your big problems. When you talk with God about your life, he listens and helps.

GOD'S PROMISE TO YOU Not a single sparrow can fall to the ground without your Father knowing it. And the very hairs on your head are all numbered. So don't be afraid; you are more valuable to God than a whole flock of sparrows. MATTHEW 10:29-31

God, I'm unsure of how to ask for your help. How should I talk to you?

ANSWER FROM GOD'S WORD The Holy Spirit helps us in our weakness. For example, we don't know what God wants us to pray for. But the Holy Spirit prays for us with groanings that cannot be expressed in words. ROMANS 8:26

God gives you his Holy Spirit as your personal intercessor. When you don't know how or what to pray, the Holy Spirit will pray for you. God understands that sometimes you won't know what to ask for or how to express your feelings. He promises that you never have to worry about what to say to him. His Spirit will ask him to help you even when you don't know how to articulate the kind of help you need.

GOD'S PROMISE TO YOU When they call on me, I will answer; I will be with them in trouble. I will rescue and honor them. I will . . . give them my salvation. PSALM 91:15-16

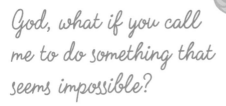

God, what if you call me to do something that seems impossible?

ANSWER FROM GOD'S WORD Now all glory to God, who is able, through his mighty power at work within us, to accomplish infinitely more than we might ask or think. EPHESIANS 3:20

God's strength shines brightest in your weakness. Jesus says, "What is impossible for people is possible with God" (Luke 18:27). The next time life throws the impossible at you, see it as an opportunity for God's power to work through your human limitations. Watch how God will help you accomplish more than you ever could have dreamed.

GOD'S PROMISE TO YOU Jesus looked at them intently and said, "Humanly speaking, it is impossible. But with God everything is possible." MATTHEW 19:26

God, how is your kind of love different from how our culture defines love?

ANSWER FROM GOD'S WORD You have heard the law that says, "Love your neighbor" and hate your enemy. But I say, love your enemies! Pray for those who persecute you! MATTHEW 5:43-44

God calls us to a radical lifestyle of loving those who are seen as unlovable. In reaching out to befriend the imperfect people God has placed in your life, you may provide the only source of love that person experiences. You may be surprised at how God can bring the most unlikely individuals together as friends. When you reach out with God's love, not only will you profoundly affect the lives of others, but your heart will be changed as well.

GOD'S PROMISE TO YOU I will show love to those I called "Not loved." And to those I called "Not my people," I will say, "Now you are my people." And they will reply, "You are our God!" HOSEA 2:23

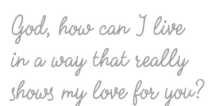

God, how can I live in a way that really shows my love for you?

ANSWER FROM GOD'S WORD Those who obey God's word truly show how completely they love him. 1 JOHN 2:5

Do you want to show how much you love God? He tells you how: Simply obey him. When you obey God, you demonstrate your belief that his ways are right and he knows what is best for you. The more you obey him, the more you will see that following God's Word really is best. You will begin to experience the joy and peace found in obedience, and you will love God even more for showing you how to live a life of fulfillment.

GOD'S PROMISE TO YOU Jesus replied, "All who love me will do what I say. My Father will love them, and we will come and make our home with each of them." JOHN 14:23

God, what is the secret to lasting and satisfying love?

ANSWER FROM GOD'S WORD Love is patient and kind. Love is not jealous or boastful or proud or rude. It does not demand its own way. It is not irritable, and it keeps no record of being wronged. It does not rejoice about injustice but rejoices whenever the truth wins out. Love never gives up, never loses faith, is always hopeful, and endures through every circumstance.
1 CORINTHIANS 13:4-7

These well-known verses are some of the most eloquent and accurate descriptions of love ever written. Contrary to popular opinion, true love is a courageous commitment and an unwavering choice to care for another person. When you love like that, feelings of satisfaction and fulfillment will often follow.

GOD'S PROMISE TO YOU Three things will last forever—faith, hope, and love—and the greatest of these is love. 1 CORINTHIANS 13:13

God, where am I most vulnerable to spiritual attack?

ANSWER FROM GOD'S WORD Put on every piece of God's armor so you will be able to resist the enemy in the time of evil. Then after the battle you will still be standing firm. EPHESIANS 6:13

Satan always strikes at your weak spots—those areas you refuse to give over to God. Pride, hard-heartedness, anger, and bitterness are areas that make you vulnerable, where you are most easily tempted. These are the joints in your spiritual armor at which the enemy takes aim. But God promises to give you the strength to overcome the attacks of Satan. Allow God to cover your weaknesses with his strength by giving him control over the areas where you are most susceptible to temptation.

GOD'S PROMISE TO YOU We know that God's children do not make a practice of sinning, for God's Son holds them securely, and the evil one cannot touch them. 1 JOHN 5:18

God, how can I extend to others the forgiveness you have shown to me?

ANSWER FROM GOD'S WORD Peter came to him and asked, "Lord, how often should I forgive someone who sins against me? Seven times?" "No, not seven times," Jesus replied, "but seventy times seven!" MATTHEW 18:21-22

Forgiveness doesn't mean that your hurt doesn't exist or doesn't matter, nor does it make everything all right. Forgiving someone allows you to let go of your hurt and allow God to deal with the one who hurt you. Forgiveness sets you free and allows you to move on. It's not always easy, but forgiving someone who has hurt you models how Jesus has forgiven you, while also releasing you from anger and bitterness.

GOD'S PROMISE TO YOU LORD, if you kept a record of our sins, who, O Lord, could ever survive? But you offer forgiveness, that we might learn to fear you. PSALM 130:3-4

God, what happens when I work for peace?

ANSWER FROM GOD'S WORD Those who are peacemakers will plant seeds of peace and reap a harvest of righteousness. JAMES 3:18

Being a peacemaker means your actions plant seeds of harmony and unity, not discord, gossip, or division. An environment of peace helps people get along, work together productively, and respect one another's differences. In every situation ask yourself, *What am I planting by my response?* Over time you will harvest the benefits of living this way with your family, friends, and neighbors. God promises to bless those who work for peace.

GOD'S PROMISE TO YOU God blesses those who work for peace, for they will be called the children of God. MATTHEW 5:9

God, can I make an impact for you at work?

ANSWER FROM GOD'S WORD God has not given us a spirit of fear and timidity, but of power, love, and self-discipline. So never be ashamed to tell others about our Lord. 2 TIMOTHY 1:7-8

Work was always meant to honor God, to give people the dignity of having something important to do, and to bring blessing to others. Work is anchored in God's very character. Part of being made in God's image is sharing in the industrious and creative aspects of his nature. Gardening was the very first job humans had. Christians are needed in all kinds of vocations. Whatever your job, believe that God has placed you there for a reason, and then do your work well as a service to God and as a way to allow others to see his love in action through you. The quality of your work and your enthusiasm for it reveal the nature of your commitment to Jesus.

GOD'S PROMISE TO YOU Work willingly at whatever you do, as though you were working for the Lord rather than for people. Remember that the Lord will give you an inheritance as your reward. COLOSSIANS 3:23-24

God, do you open doors of opportunity for me, or do things just happen by chance?

ANSWER FROM GOD'S WORD I want you to know, my dear brothers and sisters, that everything that has happened to me here has helped to spread the Good News. PHILIPPIANS 1:12

Sometimes it's hard to tell whether life's events are coincidence or part of God's plan. If everything happens merely by chance, then either there is no God at all or God is impersonal and detached. The Bible says that not only is God real, but he is also compassionate and deeply involved in his creation. You may not understand how certain events in your life fit into God's plan, but you can be confident that God is watching over you and guiding you in a specific direction.

GOD'S PROMISE TO YOU We may throw the dice, but the LORD determines how they fall. PROVERBS 16:33

God, how important are integrity and good character?

ANSWER FROM GOD'S WORD The LORD rewarded me for doing right. He has seen my innocence. To the faithful you show yourself faithful; to those with integrity you show integrity. PSALM 18:24-25

Integrity means knowing what you believe and living as if you believe it. You build a reputation of integrity over time as you consistently demonstrate your honest dependability through your words and actions. This involves being faithful in every area of your life, no matter how small. In fact, it's often in the little things that your integrity will be tested the most. What you do day by day forges your lasting reputation. Your actions moment by moment establish the personal qualities for which you will be remembered. At some point, you will find yourself or someone you love in a desperate situation, and you will realize that your integrity is the only thing that will save the day. Others will look to you to do the right thing, and you will thank God that your integrity created a divine moment.

GOD'S PROMISE TO YOU I know, my God, that you examine our hearts and rejoice when you find integrity there. 1 CHRONICLES 29:17

God, what should I do while I'm waiting for your guidance?

ANSWER FROM GOD'S WORD Be still in the presence of the LORD, and wait patiently for him to act. Don't worry about evil people who prosper or fret about their wicked schemes. . . . For the wicked will be destroyed, but those who trust in the LORD will possess the land. PSALM 37:7, 9

The faithful servants in Jesus' parable of stewardship were praised for serving while the master was gone. Sometimes we fall into the habit of expecting others to take care of our needs while we wait for God to show us his will, but that causes us to focus on ourselves. While you wait, serve God and others, because while you are serving you will receive your next assignment from God. You can be confident that God wants you to serve him faithfully right where you are while you wait to find out what he wants you to do next.

GOD'S PROMISE TO YOU He will be gracious if you ask for help. He will surely respond to the sound of your cries. . . . Right behind you a voice will say, "This is the way you should go," whether to the right or to the left. ISAIAH 30:19, 21

God, how can I know that you value me?

ANSWER FROM GOD'S WORD God showed how much he loved us by sending his one and only Son into the world so that we might have eternal life through him. This is real love—not that we loved God, but that he loved us and sent his Son as a sacrifice to take away our sins. 1 JOHN 4:9-10

What makes something valuable? One way to determine the value of something is to consider the price that was paid for it. Other considerations include the object's uniqueness and its purpose. When God created you, he uniquely designed you for a special purpose because he loves you and has a plan for you. Then he paid the ultimate price for you by sending his Son to die for you. You are immeasurably valuable to God. You are priceless!

GOD'S PROMISE TO YOU What are mere mortals that you should think about them, human beings that you should care for them? Yet you made them only a little lower than God and crowned them with glory and honor. PSALM 8:4-5

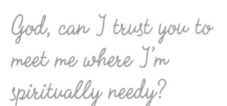

God, can I trust you to meet me where I'm spiritually needy?

ANSWER FROM GOD'S WORD Since he did not spare even his own Son but gave him up for us all, won't he also give us everything else? ROMANS 8:32

God promises he will always meet your spiritual needs for salvation, mercy, wisdom, comfort, strength, a way out of temptation, and faith. He meets these needs through the Holy Spirit living in you. Your needs are opportunities to experience God's provision and compassion. He doesn't expect you to figure it out on your own, but he loves meeting you where you are, to provide his loving assistance. If he gave up his Son for you, you can trust him to provide everything else you need as well.

GOD'S PROMISE TO YOU Fear the LORD, you his godly people, for those who fear him will have all they need. PSALM 34:9

God, how can I be a good steward of what you have given me?

ANSWER FROM GOD'S WORD Whether we are here in this body or away from this body, our goal is to please him. 2 CORINTHIANS 5:9

The goal of stewardship is to make the best possible use of what you have so that God's work can move forward as efficiently and effectively as possible. You are ultimately accountable to God for how you use your gifts and opportunities, whether for yourself or for the benefit of others. God entrusts you with certain resources and abilities and then expects you to maximize them through wise and godly stewardship. God promises to reward you if you use well what he has entrusted to you.

GOD'S PROMISE TO YOU If the master returns and finds that the servant has done a good job, there will be a reward. MATTHEW 24:46

God, how can I gain a spiritual heritage?

ANSWER FROM GOD'S WORD   The Spirit is God's guarantee that he will give us the inheritance he promised and that he has purchased us to be his own people. EPHESIANS 1:14

You can't choose the family you were born into, but you can choose a spiritual heritage by joining the family of God. You can enjoy the witness and wisdom of those who have faithfully served God in the past, as well as the very presence and power of God himself in the form of the Holy Spirit. All those who believe in Jesus Christ are God's children. If you love him, obey him, and worship him, he promises to give you an eternal inheritance.

GOD'S PROMISE TO YOU   His salvation extends to the children's children of those who are faithful to his covenant, of those who obey his commandments! PSALM 103:17-18

God, what can motivate me to grow in generosity?

ANSWER FROM GOD'S WORD If you give even a cup of cold water to one of the least of my followers, you will surely be rewarded.
MATTHEW 10:42

One of the unique promises of the Bible is that the more you give, the more you receive—not necessarily in material possessions, but in spiritual and eternal rewards. This is a truth that can be learned only when put into practice. Through generous giving, you learn to trust God to meet your needs and bless others through you. Your monetary investments will be worthless to you when you die—you can't take them with you. But any spiritual investments you make now will reward you with eternal payoffs.

GOD'S PROMISE TO YOU Give, and you will receive. LUKE 6:38

God, what does it mean to be righteous?

ANSWER FROM GOD'S WORD Throw off your old sinful nature and your former way of life, which is corrupted by lust and deception. Instead, let the Spirit renew your thoughts and attitudes. Put on your new nature, created to be like God— truly righteous and holy. . . . Create in me a clean heart, O God. Renew a loyal spirit within me. EPHESIANS 4:22-24; PSALM 51:10

If you have faith in God and believe that Jesus died for your sins and was raised to eternal life, you are "made right" in God's eyes. You don't have to be perfect to be righteous. God is looking for your faith and your willingness to follow him. Those who are righteous, or godly, in God's eyes are safe in his care—their souls are secure for eternity. You have the courage to do the right thing and are not ashamed of your faith; you are persistent in prayer and enjoy close fellowship with God. When you live like this, others can see you are different, and they will be attracted to the godly qualities they see in you.

GOD'S PROMISE TO YOU Surely righteous people are praising your name; the godly will live in your presence. PSALM 140:13

God, how can I trust that what the Bible says is true?

ANSWER FROM GOD'S WORD You must realize that no prophecy in Scripture ever came from the prophet's own understanding, or from human initiative. No, those prophets were moved by the Holy Spirit, and they spoke from God. 2 PETER 1:20-21

When you first believed that Jesus died to save you, and you gave your heart and soul to him, you took a leap of faith. Believing that the Bible is true is another leap of faith. But once you start to read and explore it, you will be convinced it is God's truth, because it will speak to every situation you face, every thought you think, and every emotion you feel. You will come to see that it is "alive and powerful," meaning that it is relevant and personal to your unique situation. Your leap of faith will land you on the rock of solid truth that God's Word is reliable and pertinent to every facet of your life.

GOD'S PROMISE TO YOU The grass withers and the flowers fade, but the word of our God stands forever. ISAIAH 40:8

God, why do you discipline me?

ANSWER FROM GOD'S WORD The Lord corrects those he loves, just as a father corrects a child in whom he delights. PROVERBS 3:12

A life without discipline has no focus, no purpose, no direction, no boundaries. God's discipline is an act of love to guide you back to him. Left to ourselves, we tend to move toward an unfocused and unhealthy life, and thus away from God. God's discipline reminds us of his care for us and how he longs to see us grow to maturity. He promises that the ultimate result of his discipline will be blessing.

GOD'S PROMISE TO YOU Joyful are those you discipline, Lord, those you teach with your instructions. PSALM 94:12

God, how am I supposed to love my enemies?

Bless those who persecute you. Don't curse them; pray that God will bless them. Be happy with those who are happy, and weep with those who weep. Live in harmony with each other. . . . Never pay back evil with more evil. Do things in such a way that everyone can see you are honorable. Do all that you can to live in peace with everyone.
ROMANS 12:14-18

Does the word *enemy* bring to mind a particular person? Forgiveness and love might be far from your thoughts when you envision this person, but those are exactly the responses Jesus calls you to. When you love your enemy, you see that person as Christ does—someone in need of grace and forgiveness. When you are hurt, is your tendency to hurt back? God assures you that he sees your hurt, he is the judge, and he will help you deal in the right way with those who hurt you.

GOD'S PROMISE TO YOU If your enemies are hungry, feed them. If they are thirsty, give them something to drink. . . . Your love for one another will prove to the world that you are my disciples.
ROMANS 12:20; JOHN 13:35

God, how can my life be fruitful in every season?

ANSWER FROM GOD'S WORD The godly will flourish like palm trees and grow strong like the cedars of Lebanon. For they are transplanted to the LORD's own house. They flourish in the courts of our God. Even in old age they will still produce fruit; they will remain vital and green. PSALM 92:12-14

The Bible often uses metaphors of trees and vines to paint a picture of how people can be useful and productive. From your connection with God, you receive nourishment to be fruitful in every season of life. If you follow this metaphor of your life as a tree or a vine, what kind of fruit are you bearing? In other words, are others experiencing the sweet taste of God's goodness and blessing from you? The key to fruitfulness is staying connected to God, the source of your nourishment and strength.

GOD'S PROMISE TO YOU I am the vine; you are the branches. Those who remain in me, and I in them, will produce much fruit. JOHN 15:5

God, is hoping for heaven just wishful thinking?

ANSWER FROM GOD'S WORD This world is not our permanent home; we are looking forward to a home yet to come. . . . We are looking forward to the new heavens and new earth he has promised, a world filled with God's righteousness.
HEBREWS 13:14; 2 PETER 3:13

Feeling disappointed with this world isn't meant to lead to feelings of hopelessness. It is meant to grow our hope and desire for heaven. We sense that things in this world aren't always as they should be. God promises that in heaven everything will be made right again, as it was when he first created the world. Does it sound too good to be true? It's too good to miss! Your longing for something more is your inbuilt desire for an unbroken relationship with the almighty and all-loving God.

GOD'S PROMISE TO YOU This world is fading away, along with everything that people crave. But anyone who does what pleases God will live forever. 1 JOHN 2:17

God, who is Jesus? And why should I believe in him?

ANSWER FROM GOD'S WORD These are written so that you may continue to believe that Jesus is the Messiah, the Son of God, and that by believing in him you will have life by the power of his name. JOHN 20:31

Jesus Christ is the Son of God, the Savior of the world who was promised by God. He is fully God and fully human. He lived a sinless life so that he could die on the cross to take the punishment that we deserve for our sins. Then he rose from the dead to prove that he has power over death and to assure you that if you believe in him as Lord, you will also be raised to eternal life. Through Jesus, every promise of God is fulfilled, and he is the ultimate assurance that every word of God will come true.

GOD'S PROMISE TO YOU Christ is the visible image of the invisible God. He existed before anything was created and is supreme over all creation. COLOSSIANS 1:15

God, how can I connect more with you in my daily life?

ANSWER FROM GOD'S WORD Learn to know . . . God . . . intimately. Worship and serve him with your whole heart and a willing mind. For the LORD sees every heart and knows every plan and thought. If you seek him, you will find him. 1 CHRONICLES 28:9

Living for God means that in all circumstances and in every situation, you pause to acknowledge that he is in control and then act in faith that what he says is good and true. It is the most noble purpose your life could have because it brings the eternal presence and power of your Creator into your routine and everyday life. You live aware of his presence. As you learn to acknowledge him in your daily routines, you will grow more deeply connected to him.

GOD'S PROMISE TO YOU The LORD protects those of childlike faith. . . . So I walk in the LORD's presence as I live here on earth! PSALM 116:6, 9

God, with tragedies all around, can I trust you to protect me?

ANSWER FROM GOD'S WORD God's way is perfect. All the LORD's promises prove true. He is a shield for all who look to him for protection.
PSALM 18:30

The Lord is our shield and shelter: He protects, rescues, and watches over us. We must not conclude, however, that we are somehow outside of God's protection if we experience troubles. God's protection has far greater purposes than helping us avoid pain; it is to make us better servants for him. God also protects us by guiding us through painful circumstances, not always by helping us escape them. No matter how the storms of life batter you, you are eternally secure with God. He has given you the protection of his ways and his Word to keep you grounded in truth and to help you travel steadily on in faith. It's amazing to think of a God who is so aware of your need to feel secure. In what areas of life do you feel weak and vulnerable? Let the assurance of God's protection become your strength. He is your safe place, your fortress.

GOD'S PROMISE TO YOU The LORD is a shelter for the oppressed, a refuge in times of trouble.
PSALM 9:9

God, are you really in control of this chaotic world?

ANSWER FROM GOD'S WORD The LORD has made the heavens his throne; from there he rules over everything. PSALM 103:19

With all the chaos in the world today, it can feel as if your world is spinning out of control. Pain, loss, or illness can make you doubt God's goodness and engagement in your life. God has given us his Word for times such as these. God rules over everything, both the laws of nature and the kingdoms of this world. When you fear for the future, take comfort in knowing that God's love and care extend to every generation. God promises his power and authority are at work in the world at large and in your own heart as well.

GOD'S PROMISE TO YOU You, O LORD, will sit on your throne forever. Your fame will endure to every generation. PSALM 102:12

God, how can I patiently wait for your timing in my life?

ANSWER FROM GOD'S WORD When we were utterly helpless, Christ came at just the right time and died for us sinners. ROMANS 5:6

God's people had been longing for the Messiah for centuries, yet God waited until just the right time to send Jesus to earth. We may not fully understand why this timing was perfect until we get to heaven and see God's complete plan. The same is true for us in our individual lives. We may be waiting on the Lord for an answer, but we can trust that it will come at just the right time. Keep praying, be patient, and stay alert as you wait for God to reveal his purpose and his plan in his time.

GOD'S PROMISE TO YOU At just the right time, I will respond to you. On the day of salvation I will help you. ISAIAH 49:8

God, I keep struggling with the same issues. Are you still at work in me?

ANSWER FROM GOD'S WORD   I am certain that God, who began the good work within you, will continue his work until it is finally finished on the day when Christ Jesus returns. PHILIPPIANS 1:6

From the minute God begins "the good work" in you, he promises to continue working for the rest of your life, transforming every aspect of your heart and your character. He will show you how to become more like him in your relationships, work, service, and love. If you ask him to work within you every day, you will be ready when he finally takes you home to be with him forever.

GOD'S PROMISE TO YOU   God is working in you, giving you the desire and the power to do what pleases him. PHILIPPIANS 2:13

God, why do you give us freedom of choice, knowing we won't always choose wisely?

ANSWER FROM GOD'S WORD The LORD God warned him, "You may freely eat the fruit of every tree in the garden—except the tree of the knowledge of good and evil. If you eat its fruit, you are sure to die." GENESIS 2:16-17

Genuine love must allow the freedom to choose. God loves you so much that he gave you this freedom. But along with the ability to make choices comes the possibility of choosing your own way over God's way. Sin and evil exist because God's creatures have chosen their own way instead of God's. But when you choose to do what is right, God is greatly pleased. He rewards your faithfulness, and your relationship with him flourishes.

GOD'S PROMISE TO YOU Don't you realize that you become the slave of whatever you choose to obey? You can be a slave to sin, which leads to death, or you can choose to obey God, which leads to righteous living. ROMANS 6:16

God, isn't it unrealistic to expect imperfect humans to live up to your standards?

ANSWER FROM GOD'S WORD When I tried to keep the law, it condemned me. So I died to the law—I stopped trying to meet all its requirements—so that I might live for God.
GALATIANS 2:19

Sometimes it seems as if God places unrealistic expectations on us. How can we possibly obey all that he commands? God understands that these expectations are impossible, which is why he sent Jesus so that we wouldn't have to live with the burden of trying to be perfect. When God looks at you, he sees Jesus' perfect life and sacrifice on your behalf. God's greatest expectation is not that you live a perfect life, but that you love him with all your heart.

GOD'S PROMISE TO YOU I can do everything through Christ, who gives me strength.
PHILIPPIANS 4:13

God, does your voice still speak with authority today?

ANSWER FROM GOD'S WORD When Jesus woke up, he rebuked the wind and the raging waves. Suddenly the storm stopped and all was calm. LUKE 8:24

The same God whose voice instantly calmed the storm on the Sea of Galilee has the authority to speak calmness to the storms in your heart, dry up a flood of fear, quench the lust for sin, and control the whirlwind of life. God's voice has just as much power and authority today as it did in Bible times. Listen for his voice in prayer and in the Bible. Whether God's voice creates a dramatic life change or leads you on a steady walk of faith, your life can be a demonstration of God's powerful work in you.

GOD'S PROMISE TO YOU "I am the Alpha and the Omega—the beginning and the end," says the Lord God. "I am the one who is, who always was, and who is still to come—the Almighty One." REVELATION 1:8

God, can you use me to bring about greater justice in the world?

ANSWER FROM GOD'S WORD The righteous LORD loves justice. . . . O people, the LORD has told you what is good, and this is what he requires of you: to do what is right, to love mercy, and to walk humbly with your God. PSALM 11:7; MICAH 6:8

God wants us to be agents of justice in the world. Ignoring those who are exploited and oppressed puts our hearts in danger of becoming callous—and even corrupt—in relation to the needs of others. Ask God to soften your heart toward those in need. Become an advocate for those who are treated unfairly, and intercede for those who need help. You can do this by speaking up when someone is treated unjustly, helping someone financially, or offering an encouraging word or a blessing. God promises that those who work for justice will see him work in powerful ways.

GOD'S PROMISE TO YOU LORD, you know the hopes of the helpless. Surely you will hear their cries and comfort them. You will bring justice to the orphans and the oppressed, so mere people can no longer terrify them. PSALM 10:17-18

God, how can I experience more of your favor?

ANSWER FROM GOD'S WORD My child, never forget the things I have taught you. Store my commands in your heart. . . . Then you will find favor with both God and people, and you will earn a good reputation. PROVERBS 3:1, 4

What greater favor from God could there be than his personal advice on how to live? When you pursue God's wisdom, you will experience his favor, because no one can give you better advice and guidance than God. And no one else knows you as well or wants you to succeed more. God's favor is on those who treasure his wisdom and put his advice into practice.

GOD'S PROMISE TO YOU May the LORD bless you and protect you. May the LORD smile on you and be gracious to you. May the LORD show you his favor and give you his peace. NUMBERS 6:24-26

God, how can your Word guide me when I am confused?

ANSWER FROM GOD'S WORD I have tried hard to find you—don't let me wander from your commands. . . . Open my eyes to see the wonderful truths in your instructions. . . . Arrogant people smear me with lies, but in truth I obey your commandments with all my heart.
PSALM 119:10, 18, 69

Confusion comes when you believe lies about who God is and who you are. But it can also come when you lose sight of where you're going in life. With God's Word as your compass, you can be certain about which roads *not* to take, reducing much confusion in your life. God's Word brings insight and clarity by offering you wisdom, pointing you toward truth, and guiding you in the right direction.

GOD'S PROMISE TO YOU Your word is a lamp to guide my feet and a light for my path.
PSALM 119:105

God, did Jesus really have to die so we could be forgiven?

ANSWER FROM GOD'S WORD He is the one all the prophets testified about, saying that everyone who believes in him will have their sins forgiven through his name. ACTS 10:43

Sin and death go hand in hand. Though our sins may not cause us to die right away, the effects of sin will ultimately lead to death. God is the giver of life. For us to live forever with him, he knew that an ultimate sacrifice would have to be made to provide eternal atonement for sin. In his death, Jesus paid the price for sin, and his resurrection conquered death so we could receive eternal life through him.

GOD'S PROMISE TO YOU The wages of sin is death, but the free gift of God is eternal life through Christ Jesus our Lord. ROMANS 6:23

God, how can my daily Bible reading become more meaningful?

ANSWER FROM GOD'S WORD   The gracious hand of his God was on him. This was because Ezra had determined to study and obey the Law of the LORD and to teach those decrees and regulations to the people of Israel.   EZRA 7:9-10

You will have ups and downs when it comes to reading the Bible. Some days you will feel as if every word were written just for you, and other days you will feel that you just aren't hearing God speak. The key is to be consistent and faithful. Ezra knew the Scriptures because he was determined to study, obey, and teach them regularly. As you read God's Word every day, remember that it is alive and pertinent to every situation in your life.

GOD'S PROMISE TO YOU   Open my eyes to see the wonderful truths in your instructions. . . . Your laws are wonderful. No wonder I obey them! The teaching of your word gives light, so even the simple can understand.   PSALM 119:18, 129-130

God, if I forget to mention something in prayer, do you still know it's on my mind?

ANSWER FROM GOD'S WORD You know what I am going to say even before I say it, LORD.
PSALM 139:4

God knows your thoughts. That can be intimidating or comforting—depending on what you are thinking. When you pray, you don't need to go through your entire list every time. Instead, the Holy Spirit will bring to mind certain needs at certain times that you can bring to God in prayer. That doesn't mean other concerns will be overlooked. God knows what's on your heart. You can have peace, knowing that God answers not only the prayers you speak but also those you don't.

GOD'S PROMISE TO YOU Your Father knows exactly what you need even before you ask him!
MATTHEW 6:8

God, people today think that truth is relative. How can I know what is really true?

ANSWER FROM GOD'S WORD Jesus responded, "You say I am a king. Actually, I was born and came into the world to testify to the truth. All who love the truth recognize that what I say is true." "What is truth?" Pilate asked. JOHN 18:37-38

Like Pilate, many people today think that truth is whatever they want it to be; but when there is no standard for truth, there is no standard for right and wrong. The Bible says that truth exists in the person and character of God. He not only created truth, he *is* truth, so only truth can come from him. To learn what is true, read the Bible. The distinction between living by God's standards and living by your own definition of truth will become clear.

GOD'S PROMISE TO YOU You will know the truth, and the truth will set you free. JOHN 8:32

God, how do I know if an opportunity is from you?

ANSWER FROM GOD'S WORD Be careful to obey all the instructions Moses gave you. Do not deviate from them, turning either to the right or to the left. Then you will be successful in everything you do. . . . Plans go wrong for lack of advice; many advisers bring success. JOSHUA 1:7; PROVERBS 15:22

The best way to know whether an opportunity is from God is to read and meditate on his Word, and talk with him every day in prayer. The Bible will not always give specific advice on a particular opportunity, but if an opportunity contradicts God's Word or leads you away from its principles, then you can be certain it is not from God. You may also need to ask for wisdom from trustworthy, mature believers. God will give your heart peace regarding the best choice.

GOD'S PROMISE TO YOU Seek his will in all you do, and he will show you which path to take. PROVERBS 3:6

God, what is the source of temptation?

ANSWER FROM GOD'S WORD Satan disguises himself as an angel of light. . . . When you are being tempted, do not say, "God is tempting me." God is never tempted to do wrong, and he never tempts anyone else. 2 CORINTHIANS 11:14; JAMES 1:13

As a believer, you will face temptation, but it will never come from God. Temptation originates with Satan, who is always trying to get you to rebel against God and live in sin. Satan's favorite strategy is to make sin seem desirable and good and to twist God's truth into partial truths. The devil knows you well enough to know what will tempt you and where your weaknesses are. That's why you need to stay alert, pray, and realize that you are facing a clever enemy.

GOD'S PROMISE TO YOU Keep watch and pray, so that you will not give in to temptation. For the spirit is willing, but the body is weak! MATTHEW 26:41

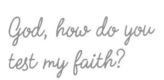

God, how do you test my faith?

ANSWER FROM GOD'S WORD Some time later, God tested Abraham's faith. . . . "This is what the LORD says: Because you have obeyed me and have not withheld even your son, your only son, I swear by my own name that I will certainly bless you." GENESIS 22:1, 16-17

As he did with Abraham, God may test you by asking you to do something hard without giving you all the information you want. God's tests are very different from Satan's temptations. God sometimes tests you to help you grow stronger and more mature in your faith. Satan tempts you to get you to sin and thus grow weaker in your faith. God may ask you to do something that requires extreme faith and obedience. He may assign you a difficult task in a very strange way, or he may delay an answer to your prayers. Through any test, God is always teaching you more about his own nature and helping your faith grow stronger.

GOD'S PROMISE TO YOU These trials will show that your faith is genuine. 1 PETER 1:7

God, what does it mean to be free in Christ?

ANSWER FROM GOD'S WORD The Lord is the Spirit, and wherever the Spirit of the Lord is, there is freedom. . . . And the Lord—who is the Spirit—makes us more and more like him as we are changed into his glorious image.
2 CORINTHIANS 3:17-18

The Bible teaches that when you believe in Jesus Christ, you become free. This means you are empowered to leave behind your sinful nature and the traps that come with it—guilt and giving in to sin, fear, and addictions. You are freed from those chains to follow God. Freedom in Christ is possible because sin has ultimately been defeated by Christ's death and resurrection. Sin no longer has power over you.

GOD'S PROMISE TO YOU If the Son sets you free, you are truly free. JOHN 8:36

God, why is it best to obey you?

ANSWER FROM GOD'S WORD [Jesus] said to Simon, "Now go out where it is deeper, and let down your nets to catch some fish." "Master," Simon replied, "we worked hard all last night and didn't catch a thing. But if you say so, I'll let the nets down again." And this time their nets were so full of fish they began to tear! LUKE 5:4-6

Simon Peter and the other fishermen had fished all night and caught nothing. Then along came Jesus, asking them to try again. Peter knew the fish weren't biting, but something about Jesus' instruction made Peter row back out onto the lake and obey, resulting in a miracle. The Bible records all that Jesus asks us to do. If we obey his instructions, we will enjoy a life of God's fullest blessings.

GOD'S PROMISE TO YOU If you look carefully into the perfect law that sets you free, and if you do what it says and don't forget what you heard, then God will bless you for doing it. JAMES 1:25

God, how much faith must I have?

ANSWER FROM GOD'S WORD It was by faith that Abraham obeyed when God called him to leave home and go to another land that God would give him as his inheritance. He went without knowing where he was going. HEBREWS 11:8

Faith is not a matter of size or quantity. Abraham believed and obeyed. Did he worry? Did he doubt? Did he second-guess himself at times? Probably. But his radical faith led him to live a radical life that was absolutely committed to God. It is not the size of your faith but the size of the *object* of your faith—the one in whom you believe—that makes the difference.

GOD'S PROMISE TO YOU I tell you the truth, if you had faith even as small as a mustard seed, you could say to this mountain, "Move from here to there," and it would move. Nothing would be impossible. MATTHEW 17:20

God, how do you prepare me for what you have in store for me?

ANSWER FROM GOD'S WORD If you keep yourself pure, you will be a special utensil for honorable use. Your life will be clean, and you will be ready for the Master to use you for every good work. 2 TIMOTHY 2:21

God's Spirit prepares us for future opportunities through today's circumstances. The key to recognizing his work in your life is to obey God's clear instructions for living, which are given in the Bible, God's Word for you. If you follow God in simple obedience where you are today, you will walk through the doors of opportunity that he opens for you in the future. The Holy Spirit uses your faithfulness today to prepare you for all the good things he has planned for you tomorrow.

GOD'S PROMISE TO YOU If I ride the wings of the morning, if I dwell by the farthest oceans, even there your hand will guide me, and your strength will support me. PSALM 139:9-10

SCRIPTURE INDEX